Cycling in the
East of England

Vincent Cassar

Commissioning Editor: Paul Mitchell
Senior Editor: Donna Wood
Senior Designer: Phil Barfoot
Copy Editor: Helen Ridge
Proofreader: Jennifer Wood
Picture Researchers: Lesley Grayson (AA)
and Jonathan Bewley (Sustrans)
Image retouching and internal repro:
Sarah Montgomery and James Tims
Cartography provided by the Mapping Services
Department of AA Publishing from data provided by
Richard Sanders and Sustrans mapping team
Research and development by: Lindsey Ryle, Melissa
Henry, Julian Hunt, Nigel Brigham and Sustrans'
regional staff
Supplementary text: Nick Cotton
Production: Lorraine Taylor

 This product includes mapping
data licensed from the Ordnance
Survey® with the permission of the Controller of Her
Majesty's Stationery Office. © Crown Copyright 2010.
All rights reserved. Licence number 100021153.

Produced by AA Publishing
© Copyright AA Media Limited 2010
ISBN: 978-0-7495-6171-0 and
(SS) 978-0-7495-6529-9

Published by AA Publishing (a trading name of
AA Media Limited, whose registered office is
Fanum House, Basing View, Basingstoke
RG21 4EA; registered number 06112600).

A04068

Free cycling permits are required on some British
Waterways canal towpaths. Visit www.waterscape.com
or call 0845 671 5530.

The National Cycle Network has been made possible
by the support and co-operation of hundreds of
organisations and thousands of individuals, including:
local authorities and councils, central governments
and their agencies, the National Lottery, landowners,
utility and statutory bodies, countryside and
regeneration bodies, the Landfill Communities Fund,
other voluntary organisations, Charitable Trusts and
Foundations, the cycle trade and industry, corporate
sponsors, community organisations and Sustrans'
Supporters. Sustrans would also like to extend thanks
to the thousands of volunteers who generously
contribute their time to looking after their local
sections of the Network.

We have taken all reasonable steps to ensure that
the cycle rides in this book are safe and achievable
by people with a reasonable level of fitness. However,
all outdoor activities involve a degree of risk and the
publishers accept no responsibility for any injuries
caused to readers while following these cycle rides.

The contents of this book are believed correct at the
time of printing. Nevertheless, the publishers cannot
be held responsible for any errors or omissions or for
changes in the details given in this book or for the
consequences of any reliance on the information
provided by the same. This does not affect your
statutory rights.

Printed and bound in Dubai by Oriental Press
theAA.com/shop

Sustrans
2 Cathedral Square
College Green
Bristol BS1 5DD
www.sustrans.org.uk

Sustrans is a Registered Charity in the UK:
Number 326550 (England and Wales)
SCO39263 (Scotland).

CONTENTS

Foreword by Sir John Sulston   4

Introduction   6

National Cycle Network facts & figures   8

Locator map   9

Cycling with children   10

Hot tips & cool tricks   12

Bike maintenance   13

THE RIDES

1	Watford to Rickmansworth & Colne Valley	14
2	St Albans to Ware	18
3	Hertfordshire Greenways	22
4	Lee Valley	26
5	Harlow to Moreton	30
6	Chelmsford Station to Chelmer Village & Newney Green	34
7	Luton to Dunstable & Sewell Greenway	38
8	Leighton Buzzard to Bletchley	42
9	Arlesey to Letchworth Garden City & Letchworth Greenway	46
10	Flitch Way	50
11	Colchester to Hadleigh	54
12	Harwich to Wivenhoe & Colchester	58
13	Felixstowe to Orford	62
14	Ipswich to Woodbridge	66
15	Bedford to Sandy	70

16	Cambridge to Anglesey Abbey	74
17	Great Shelford to Waterbeach via Cambridge	78
18	Bury St Edmunds to Thurston & Stowmarket	82
19	Thetford to Watton	86
20	Ely to Wicken Fen	90
21	St Ives to Huntingdon & Grafham Water	94
22	March to Wisbech	98
23	Peterborough Green Wheel	102
24	Beccles to Lowestoft Ness	106
25	Beccles to Whitlingham Country Park	110
26	The Marriott's Way	114
27	Cycle to The Wash	118
28	Wells & Holkham Circuit	122
	Next steps	126
	Join Sustrans	127
	Acknowledgements	128

Hop on the bike –
... you get a bit o

Foreword by **Sir John Sulston,** Nobel Prize-winning scientist

"More and more these days we go for rides on the National Cycle Network, and what a joy that is"

We've always had bikes. How else do kids growing up in the London suburbs get around? And now – need to pop down to the shop for a pint of milk? Hop on the bike – it's fast and unobtrusive and you get a bit of exercise too. We always commute by bike, avoiding the uncertainty of traffic congestion and the hassle of parking. More and more these days we go for rides on the National Cycle Network, and what a joy that is.

One day we took the train south to Stansted, rode by the bridlepaths over the fields and round the end of the runway by tunnels and bridges to join the old railway. We contrasted our narrow track and small machines with the big jets roaring above us as they climbed out, reflecting that a free world is great, but it can't go on like this.

We lingered in the copses and glades of Hatfield Forest, and came across, for the first time, the miniature charm of Laetitia Houblon's shell house. Back to the railway path and on along the gentle slopes and curves, through the avenues of trees no longer cut far back, a pub in Dunmow, and so to Braintree by the Flitch. It was late now, but it was a grand evening as we turned our wheels to the west again and so came back to Stansted in the gathering gloom.

When I fly, as regrettably sometimes happens, I love coming home over the North Sea to East Anglia, picking up the line of coast with the familiar estuaries. Somewhere beyond is our

it's fast and ...
exercise too

section of Route 1, heading north through Essex, along the lovely Marriott's Way out of Norwich, and on around the Wash into Lincolnshire. The Network isn't visible; it hides demurely, but looking down I know it's there, carrying people around safely and blamelessly. I dream of being on it more and up above less.

Route 11 passes our house, and we use it all the time. The busy direction into Cambridge is the genome path with its coloured stripes that celebrate both DNA and the 10,000th mile of the Network. Making the stripes was an adventure. It's worked out pretty well, most people think, though one cyclist was heard to say, as he passed the stripes being laid, "What a **** waste of time!". That's the way of art, though, isn't it? Waste of time, nothing to show for it – except thoughts that are changed, moved, inspired sometimes. I think the art is a tremendous addition to the Network. We all grumble about some of it, but all have our favourite items. Art is eclectic – as strange and diverse as folk.

Of course, Cambridge is easy riding; after all, it's the cycling capital of Britain. But even here, too many people are inhibited from cycling because they feel it's risky. We need to keep pushing on the street engineering so that everyone can feel good and secure.

Happy cycling!

"I think the art is a tremendous addition to the Network"

John Sulston

INTRODUCTION

In recent years, the East of England has quite rightly been hailed as perfect cycling country, with its open skies, flat landscape and dry weather. There is no denying that the hills are gentler and the skies more welcoming, and it really is the driest (and sunniest!) region in the land.

Stranded boats at
Wells-Next-the-Sea

This guide takes you from the university city of Cambridge and the patchwork of pines at Thetford Forest to the drained flatland of the fens, through a mixture of dramatic skies with spectacular views to quaint villages lost in wooded valleys. You can cycle over ancient byways, through the grounds of stately homes or along the beach. There are miles of quiet lanes to explore, numerous delightful villages to discover and a whole host of castles, churches and ancient monuments to visit.

Much of the East of England has preserved its character, rural landscape, architecture and traditions. Evidence of its important place in history can be seen all around, from the first invasion by the Romans in 43 AD to the last attempted one at Felixstowe in 1667, this time by the Dutch. The Romans stayed for 400 years

and were the first to attempt to drain the Fens. They made Colchester the capital of Britain. The reconstructed Anglo-Saxon village at West Stow (near Bury St Edmunds) provides a good example of life in the Dark Ages; Sutton Hoo (near Woodbridge) is the famous royal burial site of Anglo-Saxon kings; while Ipswich is England's oldest continuously settled Anglo-Saxon town.

From Watford to the Wash, through the counties of Bedfordshire, Cambridgeshire, Essex, Hertfordshire, Norfolk and Suffolk, via ferries and forests, through meadows and plains, on dismantled train tracks and converted canal beds, over bridges and under arches, there is much to experience. You can connect with the bleak grandeur of Lowestoft Ness, embrace the glorious Suffolk (and north

Ely Cathedral ceiling

Reed beds in the
Norfolk Broads

Attractive street in
Great Dunmow

Essex) countryside that has inspired the likes of Gainsborough and Constable, join the birdwatchers that flock to the Norfolk coastline, or seek out the colonies of seals basking on the sandbanks at Blakeney Point.

Closer to London, there is the River Lea route, as well as Epping Forest, that green lung of London, to enjoy. You can pootle along the Grand Union Canal towpath from Leighton Buzzard to Bletchley, delight in the garden cities of Letchworth and Welwyn, and discover some artistic gems in Harlow, which has over 100 public sculptures by artists from Auguste Rodin to Henry Moore. Some of the oldest architecture to the best of the newest is to be found in this region, from the Jacobean splendour of Anglesey Abbey in Cambridge to Norman Foster's award-winning Willis Corroon

Building in Ipswich, which has the distinction of being the first building from the 1970s to become listed.

The National Cycle Network has it all covered, with 75 per cent of the UK population never more than 2 miles (3km) from a cycle track. In the East of England, there are miles and miles of splendid walking and cycling routes, with many of them completely traffic-free, which makes them perfect for everyone, including families and those new to cycling. Twenty-eight carefully chosen routes through some of the most spectacular sights in the Eastern quarter of the land are given within this guide, each one starting with a brief introduction, followed by a rundown of local attractions and nearby places to visit as well as a description of the route.

NATIONAL CYCLE NETWORK FACTS & FIGURES

Most of the routes featured here are part of the National Cycle Network. The aim of this book is to enable you to sample some of the highlights of the region on two wheels, but the rides given here are really just a taster, as there are more than 12,000 miles of Network throughout the UK to explore. More than three-quarters of us live within two miles of one of the routes.

Over a million journeys a day are made on the Network; for special trips like days out and holiday rides, but also everyday trips; taking people to school, to work, to the shops, to visit each other and to seek out green spaces. Half of these journeys are made on foot and half by bike, with urban traffic-free sections of the Network seeing the most usage.

The National Cycle Network is host to one of the UK's biggest collections of public art. Sculptures, benches, water fountains, viewing points and award-winning bridges enhance its pathways, making Sustrans one of the most prolific commissioners of public art in the UK.

The Network came into being following the award of the first-ever grant from the lottery, through the Millennium Commission, in 1995. Funding for the Network also came from bike retailers and manufacturers through the Bike Hub, as well as local authorities and councils

UK-wide, and Sustrans' many supporters. Over 2,500 volunteer Rangers give their time to Sustrans to assist in the maintenance of the National Cycle Network by adopting sections of route in communities throughout the UK. They remove glass and litter, cut back vegetation and try to ensure routes are well signed.

Developing and maintaining the National Cycle Network is just one of the ways in which Sustrans pursues its vision of a world in which people can choose to travel in ways that benefit their health and the environment.

We hope that you enjoy using this book to explore the paths and cycleways of the National Cycle Network and we would like to thank the many hundreds of organisations who have worked with Sustrans to develop the walking and cycling routes, including every local authority and council in the UK.

MAP LEGEND

Traffic Free/On Road route

Ride Start or Finish Point

National Cycle Network (Traffic Free)

National Cycle Network (On Road)

AA recommended pub	Farm or animal centre
Abbey, cathedral or priory	Garden
Abbey, cathedral or priory in ruins	Hill-fort
Aquarium	Historic house
Aqueduct or viaduct	Industrial attraction
Arboretum	Marina
Battle site	Monument
Bird Reserve (RSPB)	Museum or gallery
Cadw (Welsh Heritage) site	National Nature Reserve: England, Scotland, Wales
Campsite	Local nature reserve
Caravan site	National Trust property
Caravan & campsite	National Trust for Scotland property
Castle	Picnic site
Cave	Roman remains
Country park	Steam railway
English Heritage site	

Theme park	
Tourist Information Centre	
Viewpoint	
Visitor or heritage centre	
World Heritage Site (UNESCO)	
Zoo or wildlife collection	
AA golf course	
Stadium	
Indoor Arena	
Tennis	
Horse racing	
Rugby Union	
Football	
Athletics	
Motorsports	
County cricket	

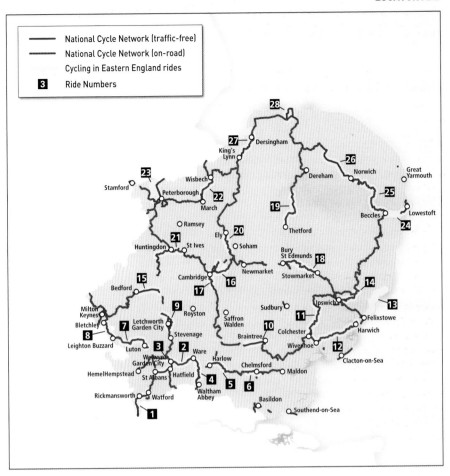

	National Cycle Network (traffic-free)
	National Cycle Network (on-road)
	Cycling in Eastern England rides
3	Ride Numbers

KEY TO LOCATOR MAP

1 Watford to Rickmansworth & Colne Valley
2 St Albans to Ware
3 Hertfordshire Greenways
4 Lee Valley
5 Harlow to Moreton
6 Chelmsford Station to Newney Green
7 Luton to Dunstable & Sewell Greenway
8 Leighton Buzzard to Bletchley
9 Arlesey to Letchworth Garden City & Letchworth Greenway
10 Flitch Way
11 Colchester to Hadleigh
12 Harwich to Wivenhoe & Colchester
13 Felixstowe to Orford
14 Ipswich to Woodbridge
15 Bedford to Sandy
16 Cambridge to Anglesey Abbey
17 Great Shelford to Waterbeach
18 Bury St Edmunds to Thurston & Stowmarket
19 Thetford to Watton
20 Ely to Wicken Fen
21 St Ives to Huntingdon & Grafham Water
22 March to Wisbech
23 Peterborough Green Wheel
24 Beccles to Lowestoft Ness
25 Beccles to Whitlingham Country Park
26 The Marriott's Way
27 Cycle to The Wash
28 Wells & Holkham Circuit

CYCLING WITH CHILDREN

Kids love bikes and love to ride. Cycling helps them to grow up fit, healthy and independent, and introduces them to the wider world and the adventure it holds.

TOP TIPS FOR FAMILY BIKE RIDES:

- Take along snacks, drinks and treats to keep their energy and spirit levels up.
- Don't be too ambitious. It's much better that everyone wants to go out again, than all coming home exhausted, tearful and permanently put off cycling.
- Plan your trip around interesting stops and sights along the way. Don't make journey times any longer than children are happy to sit and play at home.
- Even on a fine day, take extra clothes and waterproofs – just in case. Check that trousers and laces can't get caught in the chain when pedalling along.
- Wrap up toddlers. When a young child is on the back of a bike, they won't be generating heat like the person doing all the pedalling!
- Be careful not to pinch their skin when putting their helmet on. It's easily done and often ends in tears. Just place your forefinger between the clip and the chin.
- Ride in a line with the children in the middle of the adults. If there's only one of you, the adult should be at the rear, keeping an eye on all the children in front. Take special care at road junctions.
- Check that children's bikes are ready to ride. Do the brakes and gears work? Is the saddle the right height? Are the tyres pumped up?
- Carry some sticking plasters and antiseptic wipes – kids are far more likely to fall off and graze arms, hands or knees.
- Take a camera to record the trip – memories are made of this.

TRANSPORTING YOUNG CHILDREN ON TWO WHEELS

It's now easier than ever for you to ride your bike with young children.

- **Child seats:** *6 months to five years (one child)*. Once a baby can support its own head (usually at 6-12 months) they can be carried in a child seat. Seats are fitted mainly to the rear of the bike.
- **Trailers:** *babies to five years (up to two children)*. Young babies can be strapped into their car seat and carried in a trailer, and older children can be strapped in and protected from the wind and rain.
- **Tag-along trailer bikes:** *approx four to nine years*. Tag-alongs (the back half of a child's bike attached to the back of an adult one) allow a child to be towed while they either add some of their own pedal power or just freewheel and enjoy the ride.
- **Tow bar:** *approx four to eight years*. A tow bar converts a standard child's bike to a trailer bike by lifting their front wheel from the ground to prevent them from steering, while enabling them to pedal independently. When you reach a safe place, the tow bar can be detached and the child's bike freed.

TEACHING YOUR CHILD TO RIDE

There are lots of ways for children to develop and gain cycling confidence before they head out on their own.

- **Tricycles or trikes:** available for children from ten months to five years old. They have pedals so kids have all the fun of getting around under their own steam.
- **Balance bikes:** are like normal bikes but without the pedals. This means children learn to balance, steer and gain confidence on two wheels while being able to place their feet firmly and safely on the ground.

- **Training wheels:** stabilisers give support to the rear of the bike and are the easiest way to learn to ride but potentially the slowest.

BUYING THE RIGHT BIKE FOR YOUR CHILD

Every child develops differently and they may be ready to learn to ride between the ages of three and seven. When children do progress to their own bike, emphasising the fun aspect will help them take the tumbles in their stride. Encouragement and praise are important to help them persevere.

Children's bikes generally fall into age categories based on the average size of a child of a specific age. There are no hard and fast rules, as long as your child isn't stretched and can reach the brakes safely and change gear easily. It's important to buy your child a bike that fits them rather than one they can grow into. Ask your local bike shop for advice and take your child along to try out different makes and sizes.

To find a specialist cycle retailer near you visit www.thecyclingexperts.co.uk

HOT TIPS & COOL TRICKS...

WHAT TO WEAR

For most of the rides featured in this book you do not need any special clothing or footwear. Shoes that are suitable for walking are also fine for cycling. Looser-fitting trousers allow your legs to move more freely, while tops with zips let you regulate your temperature. In cold weather, take gloves and a warm hat; it's also a good idea to pack a waterproof. If you are likely to be out at dusk, take a bright reflective top. If you start to cycle regularly, you may want to invest in some specialist equipment for longer rides, especially padded shorts and gloves.

WHAT TO TAKE

For a short ride, the minimum you will need is a pump and a small tool bag with a puncture repair kit, just in case. However, it is worth considering the following: water bottle, spare inner tube, 'multi-tool' (available from cycle shops), lock, money, sunglasses, lightweight waterproof (some pack down as small as a tennis ball), energy bars, map, camera and a spare top in case it cools down or to keep you warm when you stop for refreshments.

HOW TO TAKE IT

Rucksacks are fine for light loads but can make your back hot and sweaty. For heavier loads and for longer or more regular journeys, you are better off with panniers that attach to a bike rack.

BIKE ACCESSORIES

You may also want to invest in a helmet. A helmet will not prevent accidents from happening but can provide protection if you do fall off your bike. They are particularly recommended for young children. Ultimately, wearing a helmet is a question of individual choice and parents need to make that choice for their children.

A bell is a must for considerate cyclists. A friendly tinkle warns that you are approaching, but never assume others can hear you.

LOCKING YOUR BIKE

Unless you are sitting right next to your bike when you stop for refreshments, it is worth locking it, preferably to something immovable like a post, fence or railings (or a bike stand, of course). If nothing else, lock it to a companion's bike. Bike theft is more common in towns and cities, and if you regularly leave your bike on the streets, it is important to invest in a good-quality lock and to lock and leave your bike in a busy, well-lit location.

GETTING TO THE START OF A RIDE

The best rides are often those that you can do right from your doorstep, maximizing time on your bike and reducing travelling time. If you need to travel to the start of the ride, have you thought about catching a train?

FINDING OUT MORE – WWW.SUSTRANS.ORG.UK

Use the Sustrans website to find out where you can cycle to from home or while you are away on holiday, and browse through a whole host of other useful information.
Visit www.sustrans.org.uk

MAKING THE MOST OF YOUR BIKE

Making a few simple adjustments to your bike will make your ride more enjoyable and comfortable:

- **Saddle height:** raise or lower it so that you have good contact with your pedals (to make the most of your leg power) and so that you can always put a reassuring foot on the ground.
- **Saddle position:** getting the saddle in the right place will help you get the most from your pedal power without straining your body.
- **Handlebars:** well positioned handlebars are crucial for your comfort and important for control of your steering and brakes.

... BIKE MAINTENANCE

Like any machine, a bike will work better and last longer if you care for it properly. Get in the habit of checking your bike regularly – simple checks and maintenance can help you have hassle-free riding and avoid repairs.

- **Tools:** there are specialist tools for specific tasks, but all you need to get started are: a pump, an old toothbrush, lubricants and grease, cleaning rags, a puncture repair kit, tyre levers, allen keys, screwdrivers and spanners.

REGULAR CHECKS

- **Every week:** Check tyres, brakes, lights, handlebars and seat are in good order and tightly secured.
- **Every month:** Wipe clean and lubricate chain with chain oil.
  Wipe the dirt from wheels.
  Check tread on tyres.
  Check brake pads.
  Check gear and brake cables and make sure that gears are changing smoothly.
- **Every year:** Take your bike to an experienced mechanic for a thorough service.
- **Tip:** If in doubt, leave it to the professionals. Bike mechanics are much more affordable than car mechanics, and some will even collect the bike from your home and return it to you when all the work is done.

FIXING A PUNCTURE

Punctures don't happen often and are easy to fix yourself. If you don't fancy repairing a puncture on your journey, carry a spare inner tube and a pump so you can change the tube, then fix the puncture when you get home. If you don't mind repairing punctures when they happen, make sure you carry your repair kit and pump with you at all times. All puncture repair kits have full instructions with easy-to-follow pictures.

Alternatively, if you don't want to get your hands dirty, just visit your local bike shop and they will fix the puncture for you.

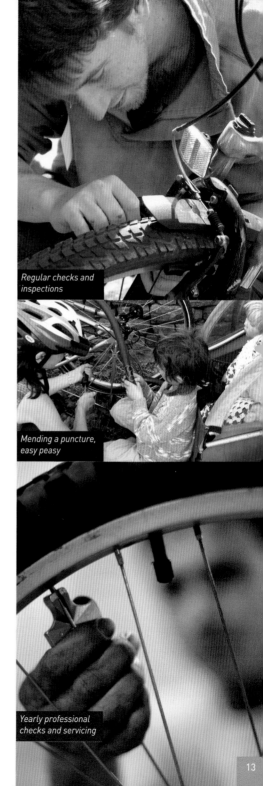

Regular checks and inspections

Mending a puncture, easy peasy

Yearly professional checks and servicing

WATFORD TO RICKMANSWORTH & COLNE VALLEY

There is plenty for cyclists to do in Hertfordshire, with a lot of disused railways now converted into cyclepaths. This walking and cycling route is a pleasant escape from the traffic and bustle of the surrounding built-up area, into a green corridor and wildlife habitat, easily accessible by all ages and abilities. It runs along the route of the former Watford to Rickmansworth railway line, which opened in 1862. The line was closed to passenger traffic in 1952 and the track dismantled 16 years later. It now forms part of National Route 61.

Rickmansworth dates back to Saxon times. With its prominent position at the confluence of three rivers – Chess, Gade and Colne – it grew to a sizeable town, gaining its royal charter in 1542. The Grand Union was built in 1797, and many businesses sprang up in the vicinity, including five paper mills and a brewery. Later, in 1862, the railway came to Watford, built by Lord Ebury. After the line finally closed in 1981, it became the Ebury Way.

Today, Rickmansworth is an attractive thriving place to live, work and shop. It is surrounded by delightful countryside, which provides a host of leisure activities.

Sculpture in Watford town centre

ROUTE INFORMATION

National Route: 6, 61
Start: Watford Junction or Watford High Street train station.
Finish: Denham Lock.
Distance: 12 miles (19.5km).
Grade: Easy.
Surface: Tarmac and fine gravel on the railway path.
Hills: None.

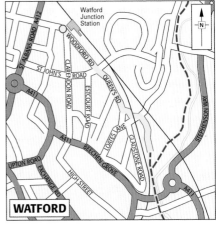

Narrowboat on the Grand Union Canal

YOUNG & INEXPERIENCED CYCLISTS

The early part of the route takes you through the centre of Watford, which can be congested, so care is needed. However, the Ebury Way is 3.5 miles (5.5km) of traffic-free cycling.

REFRESHMENTS

- Lots of choice in Watford.
- Many picnic sites on the Ebury Way.
- The Feathers pub, Rickmansworth.
- Cafe at Colne Valley Park Visitor Centre, near Denham.

THINGS TO SEE & DO

- **Croxley Common Moor**: 100-acre nature reserve and Site of Special Scientific Interest (SSSI); wonderful habitat for many different bird species, including the green woodpecker; 01992 555256
- **Batchworth Lock Canal Centre**: facilities include a gift shop and outdoor restaurant; Batchworth Ferry travels to and from Stockers Lock in a 30-minute canal trip.
- **Colne Valley Regional Park**: 43 square miles (111km sq) of countryside alongside the river, south of Rickmansworth, including woodland, farmland, farm trails, waterways, museums and aquadrome; 01895 832662; www.colnevalleypark.org.uk

TRAIN STATIONS

Watford Junction; Watford High Street; Rickmansworth (mainline and underground).

BIKE HIRE

- **Go Pedal! Bikes**: 07850 796320; www.gopedal.co.uk

FURTHER INFORMATION

- To view or print National Cycle Network routes, visit www.sustrans.org.uk
- Maps for this area are available to buy from

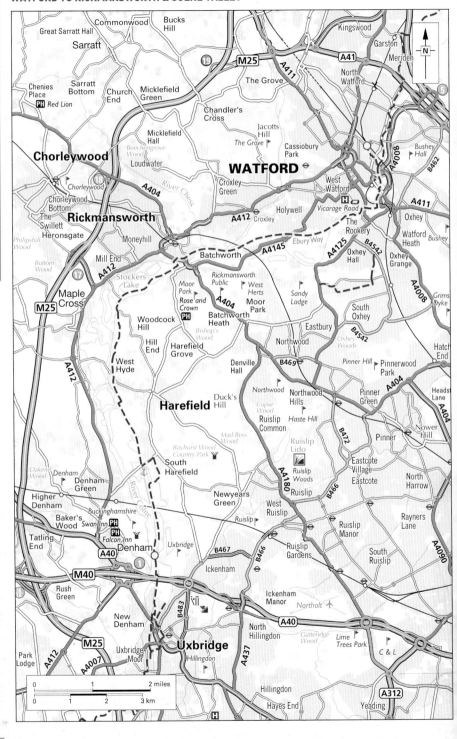

www.sustransshop.co.uk
- **Hertfordshire Tourist Information:**
  01992 584322; www.hertfordshire.com

ROUTE DESCRIPTION

From Watford Junction station, turn left onto Woodford Road and go over the roundabout onto Queen's Road. Then turn left onto Radlett Road, go under the railway bridge and take a sharp right onto Ebury Road. Bear left onto the traffic-free path, following the National Route 61 and 6 signs to Rickmansworth.

Alternatively, if you are starting from Watford High Street station, exit the station, turn right (southeast) and, after 250 metres (273 yards), turn right again to join the route.

Cycling through Watford, pass close to the Pump House Arts Centre and the Watford Arches Retail Park before passing Oxhey Playing Fields on your right. The route soon joins Wiggenhall Road as you cross the River Colne, but you return to the traffic-free path by turning right once you have crossed the river. Cross back over the river and reach Riverside Park, where children can stop and enjoy the play equipment. From here it's straight along the railway path, enjoying the greenery and keeping an eye out for local wildlife. Pass under the railway and over the Grand Union Canal, and also go by several picturesque fishing lakes. Shortly after the right-hand turn onto Skidmore Way, you can walk along the canalside footpath to the Canal Centre and shop at Batchworth Lock to find out more about the history of the Grand Union Canal.

Back on the cyclepath, you can reach Rickmansworth station and the town centre by turning right onto Church Street and following it up to the high street, turning right onto Station Road to access the station.

For Denham Lock, continue on the traffic-free section of Route 61 alongside the canal, then follow on-road and traffic-free routes.

NEARBY CYCLE ROUTES

National Route 61 goes through to Uxbridge, Slough and Windsor. Alternatively, you can extend the ride north from Watford on Route 6 to St Albans and Hatfield.

A leafy path along the Ebury Way

ST ALBANS TO WARE

This 16-mile (25.5-km) linear route joins the attractive cathedral city of St Albans to Ware at the northern end of the Lee Valley by linking two railway paths and a canal towpath. The first railway path, known as the Alban Way, runs along the former route of the Hatfield to St Albans branch line of the Great Northern Railway. All that is left of Verulamium, once the most important Roman town in Britain, lies to the west of the present city of St Albans. There are the remains of a great amphitheatre and part of an underground heating system. Modern St Albans takes its name from Alban, the first Christian martyr in Britain. The famous abbey was founded on the hill where he was beheaded. The Alban Way passes through deep wooded cuttings with occasional glimpses back to the Abbey.

A route skirting around the fringe of Welwyn Garden City takes you to the next railway path, which, at first, is open with views across arable fields but soon becomes wooded. Hertford Town's football ground comes at the end of the second railway path and the start of the urban section through the centre of Hertford, with its many refreshment stops. A short linking section between the two traffic-free rides drops you on the lovely towpath of the Lee Navigation canal, which is followed to Ware.

ROUTE INFORMATION
National Route: 61
Start: St Albans Abbey train station.

Finish: Ware train station.
Distance: 18 miles (29km).
Grade: Easy.

Surface: Tarmac and fine gravel paths.
Hills: None.

YOUNG & INEXPERIENCED CYCLISTS

The two long sections of railway path, from St Albans to Hatfield and from Welwyn Garden City to Hertford, and the Hertford to Ware towpath, are all ideal for novice riders and children. The linking sections are mainly on cycleways and quiet roads but children will need supervision, particularly at crossings.

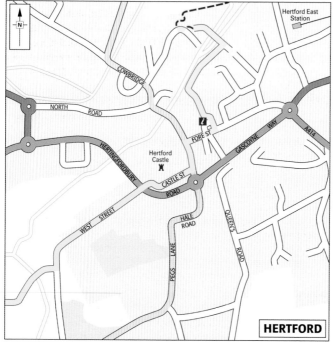

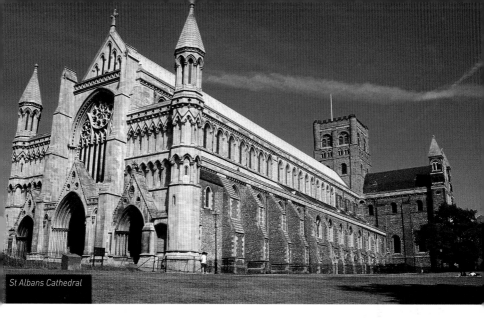

St Albans Cathedral

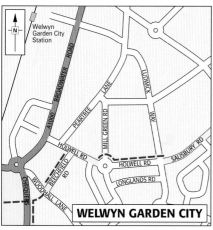

WELWYN GARDEN CITY

REFRESHMENTS

- Lots of choice just off the route in St Albans, Hatfield and Welwyn Garden City.
- Cowper Arms pub in Cole Green (between Welwyn and Hertford).
- The widest choice is in Hertford, as the route goes through the town centre.

THINGS TO SEE & DO

- Verulamium Museum and Museum of St Albans: www.stalbansmuseums.org.uk
- St Albans Abbey: founded in the 4th century; 01727 860780; www.stalbanscathedral.org.uk

- Section of Roman wall built between AD 265 and 270: to defend Verulamium; www.english-heritage.org.uk
- Hatfield House: built in 1607; the grounds include gardens, nature trails, national collection of model soldiers and the Old Palace, where Princess Elizabeth learned that she had become Queen following the death of Queen Mary in 1558. Cycles are not allowed in the grounds but you can lock your bike at the train station. 01707 287010; www.hatfield-house.co.uk
- Welwyn Garden City: one of the first garden cities, with green space extending right into the town centre.
- Hertford Castle: close to the route in the town centre; www.hertford.gov.uk

TRAIN STATIONS

St Albans Abbey; St Albans; Hatfield; Welwyn Garden City; Hertford North; Hertford East; Ware.

BIKE HIRE

Enquire locally.

FURTHER INFORMATION

- To view or print National Cycle Network routes, visit www.sustrans.org.uk

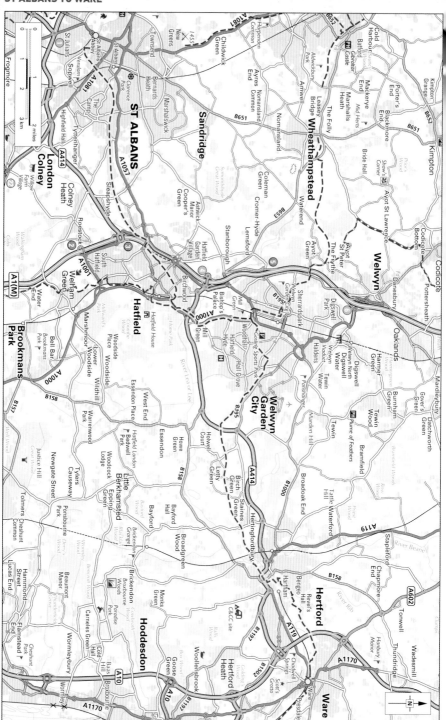

Colourful barge art can
be seen from the towpath

- Maps for this area are available to buy from
  www.sustransshop.co.uk
- **St Albans Tourist Information:** 01727 864511.

ROUTE DESCRIPTION

Leaving St Albans Abbey station, you soon join
the railway path known as the Alban Way. This
runs through deep wooded cuttings and past a
little lake before going under the mainline
railway. Continue along the route, passing
several disused platforms from the former
railway. Take care crossing the road just past
the old platform at Hill End station.

As you approach Hatfield, you pass The
Galleria shopping mall, with shops, restaurants
and leisure facilities.

A complicated but well-signposted route
around the fringe of Welwyn Garden City drops
you at the start of the second long, traffic-free
section. Hertford Town's football ground marks
the end of the railway path and the beginning of
the urban section that runs through the centre
of Hertford.

This time the link section between the two
traffic-free rides is much shorter and before
long you are on the Lee Navigation towpath,
which can be followed from Ware (beyond the
end of the ride described here) all the way into
central London.

NEARBY CYCLE ROUTES

National Route 61 goes from Windsor to the
Lee Valley; Route 12 from Hatfield to
Stevenage; and Route 6 from Watford to Luton
and Milton Keynes.

Other waymarked or traffic-free routes
include The Nickey Line, a railway path running
north from the edge of Hemel Hempstead to
Harpenden, and The Ayot Greenway, going east
from Wheathampstead to Ayot St Peter (see
page 22). The Grand Union Canal can be
followed northwest from London through
Watford and Hemel Hempstead, while the Lee
Navigation can be taken all the way south from
Ware to London (see page 26).

HERTFORDSHIRE GREENWAYS – WHEATHAMPSTEAD TO HATFIELD VILLAGE

Wheathampstead is mentioned in records from as early as 1060. Its name probably originates from 'wet homestead', which is appropriate because the early settlement was on the River Lea, with its water meadows. It has an impressive 13th-century church and is the perfect place to start this trail through Hertfordshire countryside. The route takes in part of the Ayot Greenway, and the early section is ideal for both walking and cycling, as this predominantly traffic-free route follows the former railway line that ran to Luton.

Welwyn Garden City was built soon after World War II and was the second of Ebenezer Howard's garden cities, designed to merge the best of town and country and help ease London's overcrowding. The first houses were occupied in 1920, and parts of the original settlement can be viewed by taking the Great North Way down Handside Lane.

The route ends in the new town of Hatfield, yet Hatfield village just before has many historic buildings, including the Old Palace, which was built in 1497. It was here that Princess Elizabeth learned she had become Queen of England in 1558. The Old Palace sits in the grounds of Hatfield House, a stunning Jacobean building.

ROUTE INFORMATION
National Route: 57, 12, 61
Start: Station Road, Wheathampstead
Finish: Hatfield train station.
Distance: 8 miles (13km).
Grade: Easy.
Surface: Mixture of disused railway paths and on-road links.
Hills: None.

YOUNG & INEXPERIENCED CYCLISTS
Ayot Greenway is mostly traffic-free.

REFRESHMENTS
- Lots of choice in Welwyn Garden City and Hatfield.

THINGS TO SEE & DO
- Devil's Dyke and The Slad, Wheathamstead: massive earthworks that date back to 100

WHEATHAMPSTEAD

WELWYN GARDEN CITY

St Helen's in Wheathampstead

BC; www.hertfordshire.com

- **Ayot St Peter Church:** exceptional Arts & Crafts church built in 1875; the churchyard of the earlier church can be seen a little way to the north; 01438 714150; www.welhat.gov.uk

Welwyn Garden City:

- **Welwyn Roman Baths:** scheduled ancient monument, ingeniously preserved in a steel vault under the A1(M) motorway; 01707 357117; www.welhat.gov.uk
- **Sherrardspark Woods:** 200-acre wood with walks and trails through oak and hornbeam trees; 01707 375216; www.welhat.gov.uk

Hatfield:

- **Hatfield House:** Jacobean house in its own Great Park, with magnificent gardens and nature trails; cycles are not allowed in the grounds but you can lock your bike at the train station; 01707 287010; www.hatfield-house.co.uk
- **De Havilland Aircraft Heritage Centre:** variety of complete aircraft on display, ranging from the Mosquito and Tiger Moth to modern military and civil jets; notable collection of memorabilia. Open spring and summer only, near j22 M25; 01727 826400; www.dehavillandmuseum.co.uk

TRAIN STATIONS

Welwyn Garden City; Hatfield.

BIKE HIRE

None locally.

FURTHER INFORMATION

- To view or print National Cycle Network routes, visit www.sustrans.org.uk
- Maps for this area are available to buy from www.sustransshop.co.uk
- Welwyn Garden City Tourist Information: 01707 357000; www.welhat.gov.uk

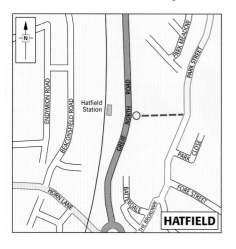

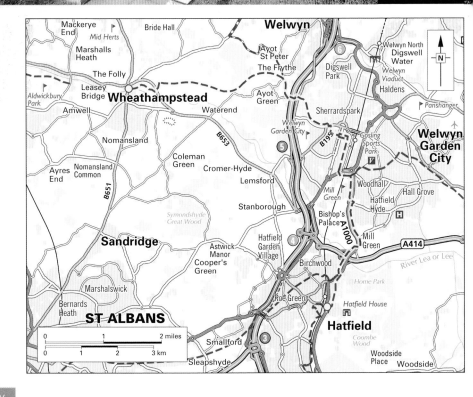

Hatfield House

Hatfield House gardens

ROUTE DESCRIPTION

From Station Road, turn into Mount Road and follow the traffic-free path, north of the river, to meet Sheepcote Lane. Turn left, crossing Cory Wright Way. Follow the signs to Ayot Green Way and for a couple of miles through a mixture of open countryside and woodland.

At Ayot Green, National Route 57 joins the Great North Way and becomes National Route 12. Cycle over the A1 through Sherrardspark Woods and into Welwyn Garden City. Follow the signposted track down Handside Lane and go east over the railway line until you head south again at the roundabout.

Follow Routes 61 and 12 south on Chequers (A1000) down to Hatfield, turning left where Route 12 leaves Route 61 on the approach to Hatfield. This route goes through Hatfield village and passes under a viaduct, which is the entrance to Hatfield House. After the viaduct, turn right through car parks and carefully make your way to Hatfield station, opposite the entrance to Hatfield House.

The Bull pub at Wheathampstead

NEARBY CYCLE ROUTES

National Route 57 goes to Hemel Hempstead via Harpenden. Route 12 runs from Hatfield to Stevenage, Route 61 from St Albans to Ware (see page 18). The Lee Navigation route can be taken all the way south from Ware to London. The 6.5-mile (10.4-km) Alban Way, a green route between Hatfield House and St Albans Abbey, is popular with walkers and cyclists due to its proximity to the town and Verulamium Park.

LEE VALLEY – WARE TO GUNPOWDER PARK

The award-winning Lee Valley Regional Park stretches an incredible 26 miles (42km) along the leafy banks of the River Lee, from Ware in Hertfordshire, through Essex, to the Thames at East India Dock Basin. This 10,000-acre park has been shaped to provide a mosaic of countryside areas, urban green spaces, country parks, nature reserves and lakeside and riverside trails. There are even sports and leisure centres sprinkled around the park.

The attractive town of Ware has been in existence since Roman times and is certainly worth looking around. The route takes you along the River Lee Country Park, and close to Waltham Abbey – a town steeped in history and dominated by the medieval abbey around which it grew.

Gunpowder Park lies just to the south of Waltham Abbey. This dynamic country park, which opened in 2004, was originally a Royal Ordnance munitions testing facility. It had been a closed site for 100 years but through a multi-million pound investment by Lee Valley Regional Park Authority (LVRPA), the land was reclaimed and regenerated. The park has been arranged into four distinct bioregions: wildflower meadows, wet willow woodland with seasonal pools, a new deciduous woodland plantation, and productive agricultural land. The Park Centre functions as a working environment to accommodate a range of free activities, including exhibitions, creative workshops and special events.

ROUTE INFORMATION

National Route: 61, 1
Start: Ware train station.
Finish: Gunpowder Park.
Distance: 13 miles (21km).
Grade: Mostly easy though there is a climb up Clayton Hill with sharp bends and a short section along Meadgate Road which has a rough surface.
Surface: Tarmac and fine gravel paths.
Hills: None, except Clayton Hill in Lee Valley Regional Park, where there are sharp Z bends on the steep ascent and descent.

YOUNG & INEXPERIENCED CYCLISTS

Except at the beginning and towards the end, the route is essentially traffic-free.

REFRESHMENTS

- Lots of choice in Ware and Waltham Abbey.
- The Fish and Eels pub, Hoddesdon.
- Cafe opposite The Fish and Eels pub, Hoddesdon.
- Lee Valley Park Farm cafe, Fishers Green.

THINGS TO SEE & DO

- **Ware:** boasts a 14th-century church, medieval manor house and many other unexpected delights; 01920 487848; www.waretourism.org.uk
- **Amwell:** former gravel pits restored to a diverse wetland nature reserve, supporting

Boats mooored on the River Lee at Ware

Lee Valley Park Farm has a dragonfly sanctuary

internationally important numbers of wintering wildfowl.

- **Rye Meads:** delightful wetland nature reserve; 01992 708383; www.rspb.org.uk
- **Rye House Gatehouse:** one of the first brick-built buildings in the country and site of the Rye House Plot, an unsuccessful attempt to assassinate King Charles II; 08456 770600; www.leevalleypark.org.uk
- **River Lee Country Park:** 1,000 acres of parkland between Waltham Abbey and Broxbourne; www.leevalleypark.org.uk
- **Lee Valley Park Farm:** consists of Hayes Hill Farm, with over 200 farm animals, including some rare breeds, and Holyfield Farm, which is a working dairy farm; 01992 892781; www.leevalleypark.org.uk
- **Waltham Abbey:** Norman church, reputedly the site of King Harold's tomb; the crypt houses a visitor centre and shop; 01992 767897; www.walthamabbeychurch.co.uk
- **Gunpowder Park:** 250 acres of regenerated green space dedicated to arts-led collaborations exploring the relationships between the public and urban and rural environments; 01992 762128; www.gunpowderpark.org

TRAIN STATIONS
Ware; St Margarets; Rye House; Broxbourne; Cheshunt; Waltham Cross.

BIKE HIRE
- **Lee Valley Cycle Hire, Broxbourne:** 01992 630127

FURTHER INFORMATION
- To view or print National Cycle Network routes, visit www.sustrans.org.uk
- Maps for this area are available to buy from www.sustransshop.co.uk
- **Lee Valley Regional Park Information Service:** 01992 702200; www.leevalleypark.org.uk

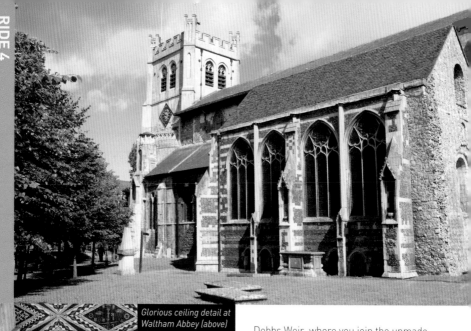

Glorious ceiling detail at Waltham Abbey (above)

Dobbs Weir, where you join the unmade Meadgate Road for a short distance before turning right, riding traffic-free once more, with views of the boating lake then fields. Go straight over the B194 Nazeing Road. Follow the shared-use path up and down Clayton Hill, being careful of the sharp Z bends, to Lee Valley Park Farm and Fishers Green. Continue through the lakes then alongside the River Lee flood relief channel before crossing the A121 at traffic lights. Continue parallel to the A121 Meridian Way and under the M25, crossing the road again to turn right at the next roundabout, then straight (across the mini-roundabout) into Gunpowder Park.

NEARBY CYCLE ROUTES

National Route 61 goes from the Lee Valley to Windsor. The route is also a part of National Route 6, between Watford and St Albans, and a part of National Route 12 between Hatfield and Welwyn Garden City (see page 22). There is a circular ride from Ware to Hertford via Brickendon, Bayford and Hoddesdon.

After Rye House station, National Route 1 continues down the Lee Valley to London, Greenwich and beyond. Lee Navigation can be taken all the way south from Waltham Abbey to London.

ROUTE DESCRIPTION

Turn right out of Ware station, go straight down Station Road and cross Viaduct Road before turning left onto Crane Mead, heading for the River Lee and joining the local towpath route. Just after Rye House station, the towpath becomes National Route 1. Follow the Lee Valley Park canal towpath, coming off just past

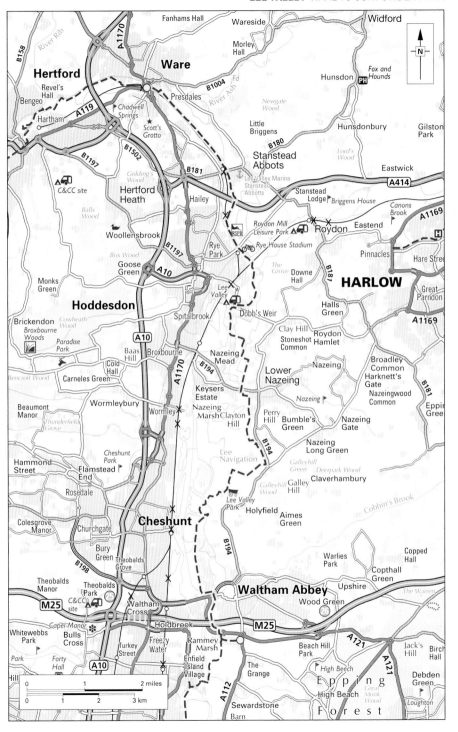

HARLOW TO MORETON

Despite its relatively modern status, Harlow has been around a long time. The new town was built after World War II to ease overcrowding in London, but there had been a Roman settlement here dating from around the third century. Archaeological excavations during the 1970s unearthed a Roman temple and a mosaic floor, which was itself built on top of an earlier Iron Age temple. The first written record of Harlow was in the Domesday Book of 1086, and what is now Old Harlow has many buildings of special architectural or historical interest.

Harlow has also labelled itself the World's First Sculpture Town. In 1947, the town's main architect, Sir Frederick Gibberd, laid down plans for Harlow to be a place where people could see great sculptures on every street corner. Now, its streets and shopping centres are home to a major collection of over 100 public sculptures by artists ranging from Auguste Rodin to Henry Moore and Barbara Hepworth. Gibberd also built up his own private collection, which can be seen in The Gibberd Garden. The garden is recognized as an important contribution to 20th-century garden design and described as 'landscape as theatre'. The whole grounds should be paid a visit.

Harlow also has one of the most extensive cycleway networks in the country, as well as its own Sculpture Heritage Trail.

ROUTE INFORMATION
National Route: 1
Start: Harlow Town station.
Finish: Church Road, Moreton (Nag's Head pub).
Distance: 8 miles (13km).
Grade: Easy.
Surface: Tarmac and fine gravel paths.
Hills: Some short hills.

YOUNG & INEXPERIENCED CYCLISTS
The route is initially off-road in Harlow, then uses quiet country lanes once you leave the town.

REFRESHMENTS
- Lots of choice in Harlow.
- Nag's Head pub, Moreton.

THINGS TO SEE & DO
- **The Gibberd Garden, Marsh Lane:** glades, groves, pools and alleys provide settings for 80 sculptures, architectural salvage, large ceramic pots, a gazebo and a moated castle; 01279 442112; www.thegibberdgarden.co.uk
- **Museum of Harlow:** tells the story of Harlow

from ancient times to the present day; situated in the picturesque former Mark Hall stable block and kitchen gardens; 01279 454959; www.harlow.gov.uk
- **Parndon Wood Nature Reserve:** ancient woodland with a fine variety of birds, mammals and insects; nature trails with hides for observing wildlife and a study centre; 01279 430005; www.visitharlow.com

'Solo Flight' by
Antanas Brazdys

'Boar' by Dame
Elizabeth Frink

'Pisces' by Jesse
Watkins

TRAIN STATIONS
Harlow Town.

BIKE HIRE
None locally.

FURTHER INFORMATION
- To view or print National Cycle Network routes, visit www.sustrans.org.uk

- Maps for this area are available to buy from www.sustransshop.co.uk
- Harlow Tourist Information: 01279 446655; www.visitharlow.com

ROUTE DESCRIPTION
From Harlow Town train station, there is a traffic-free cut-through straight ahead of you to Edinburgh Way (A414). Cross over the road and

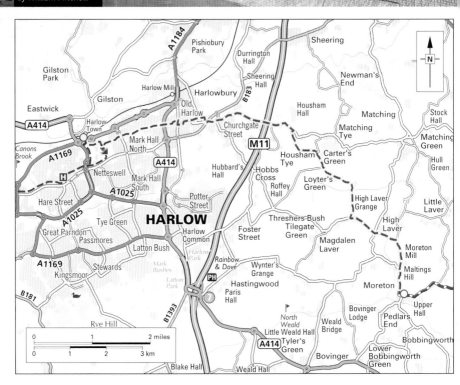

Seven reliefs/mosaics
by William Mitchell

turn left along Edinburgh Way. After a roundabout, turn right into School Lane, which has been closed to through traffic. At the junction with Park Lane turn left onto a cyclepath – a closed road that climbs up a steep hill. You then join the National Route 1 traffic-free route through the park. Using a subway, follow the path under Howard's Way and continue east on Netteswell Road, which is mostly for cyclists and pedestrians. Just after you go under the A414 and into Old Harlow, get on-road at Park Hill. When you reach Station Road, turn right then first left into Wayre Street. In the pedestrianized High Street on your left, there is cycle parking and a further sculpture.

Follow the signposts out of town and head for the M11, taking care at the crossing of Gilden Way; use the controlled crossing point. Cross over the M11 on Matching Road and take the second turning past the motorway towards High Laver. The route is fairly straightforward as you go through the village of High Laver on your way to Moreton. Stop at the Nag's Head pub for some well-earned refreshments.

NEARBY CYCLE ROUTES

National Route 1 goes east to Chelmsford and Maldon, while National Route 61 goes from Ware to St Albans (see page 18).

The plan is for National Route 11 to connect Harlow with King's Lynn in Norfolk, via Cambridge and Ely. Harlow to Stansted Mountfitchet and Waterbeach to Wicken are still under development, along with a link to Saffron Walden.

CHELMSFORD STATION TO CHELMER VILLAGE & NEWNEY GREEN

The name Chelmsford is derived from Ceolmaer's Ford, a historic crossing of the River Chelmer, situated close to where the stone bridge in the town's High Street is now. The Romans built a fort here, Caesaromagus, at the junction of the River Chelmer and the River Can, on the road linking London to Colchester. By the early 13th century, it was recognized as the county town of Essex and has remained so to this day. The Cathedral Church of St Mary the Virgin was built around 1420.

These two rides connect town to country by using Chelmsford's riverside paths alongside the River Can. To the west, Writtle has one of the loveliest village greens in Essex, with a duck pond and a backdrop of Tudor and Georgian houses. Longer rides are possible on quiet lanes leading west from Writtle through delightful undulating countryside to the pretty villages of The Rodings. These are a collection of eight villages and hamlets (Abbess, Aythorpe, Beauchamp, Berners, High, Leaden, Margaret and White Roding) located in the River Roding valley, with old churches, half-timbered cottages and moated halls.

ROUTE INFORMATION
National Route: 1
Start: Chelmsford train station
Finish: Fox and Raven pub, Chelmer Village, or the Duck Inn, Newney Green.
Distance: Chelmsford train station to Chelmer

Village 2 miles (3km). Chelmsford train station to Newney Green: 4 miles (6.5km).
Grade: Easy.
Surface: Tarmac paths and minor roads.
Hills: None.

YOUNG & INEXPERIENCED CYCLISTS
Easy-going, mainly traffic-free rides, leading to generally quiet minor roads, but care should still be taken.

Writtle village green

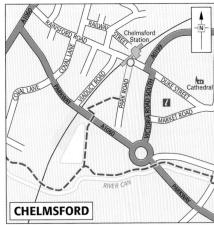

CHELMSFORD

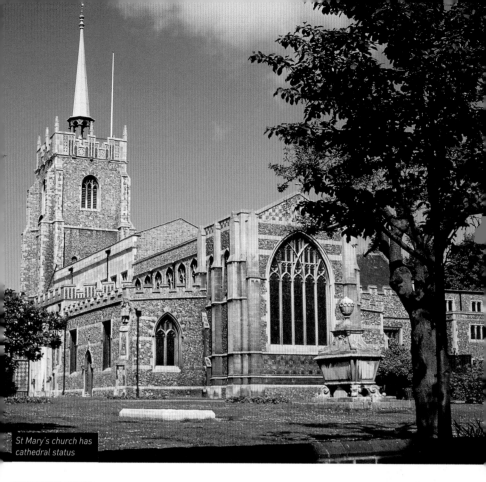

St Mary's church has cathedral status

REFRESHMENTS
- Chelmsford town centre.
- Fox and Raven pub, Chelmer Village.
- Writtle College garden centre and teashop.
- Duck Inn, Newney Green.

THINGS TO SEE & DO
- Central Park and Admiral's Park feature a lake, golf course and riverside paths.
- Old Chelmsfordians' sports field often hosts football and cricket matches.
- Chelmsford Museum: 01245 605700; www.chelmsfordbc.gov.uk/museums
- Writtle village green and duckpond.
- Hylands House and Park: best known for hosting major events and festivals but worth a visit in its own right; access through Writtle; www.chelmsford.gov.uk/hylands

TRAIN STATIONS
Chelmsford.

FURTHER INFORMATION
- To view or print National Cycle Network routes, visit www.sustrans.org.uk
- Maps for this area are available to buy from www.sustransshop.co.uk
- Chelmsford Tourist Information: 01245 283400; www.chelmsford.gov.uk

ROUTE DESCRIPTION
From Chelmsford station, cross over Duke Street and head down Park Road, turning right to cross a park and ride through a subway into Central Park.

For those wanting to head straight out to the countryside, turn right, but to explore routes

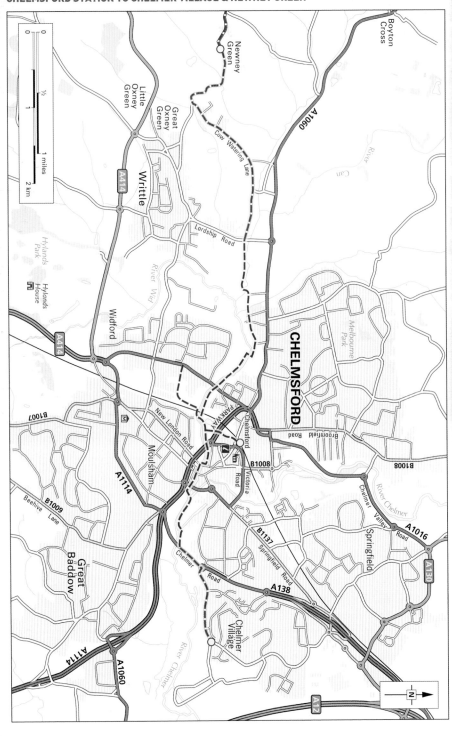

The charming old pharmacy in Writtle

through the town centre and out to Chelmer Village, turn left in Central Park and follow Route 1, past Essex County Cricket ground on your right and across the High Street. This attractive route continues along the river corridor to Chelmer Village, a relatively modern development on the edge of Chelmsford. Here, you can stop for refreshments at the Fox and Raven pub, or turn back and retrace your steps back to Central Park.

Alternatively, travelling west from Chelmsford station, follow the river through Chelmsford and out to Writtle College. Continue on Route 1 through the grounds of the college, emerging on to minor roads at the rear. The adventurous could continue on Route 1 all the way to Harlow or create their own new routes using the minor roads. The small village

of Newney Green, with its attractive Duck Inn, is the first village you come to.

NEARBY CYCLE ROUTES

National Route 13 is intended to link Chelmsford with the Thames Estuary routes further south, but the route is still in development, although it is signed through to the south of Chelmsford (see page 50).

The Flitch Way starts at Braintree, easily reached by train from Chelmsford. This forms part of Route 16 of the National Cycle Network and follows the disused railway that used to link Braintree with Bishop's Stortford.

The Wivenhoe Trail links Colchester and Wivenhoe along the River Colne corridor (see page 58). Both towns are accessible by train from Chelmsford.

LUTON TO DUNSTABLE & SEWELL GREENWAY

This ride takes you from the urban landscape of Luton to the chalk grasslands around Dunstable and along the Sewell Greenway. Luton is perhaps not the most obvious choice of destination for a day trip but it has plenty to recommend it. The selection of museums includes the Mossman collection of horse-drawn carriages and the Thomas Wyatt Bagshawe rural crafts and trades collection, both at Stockwood Park, southwest of the town centre.

The parkland along Riverside Way boasts various artworks from the Sustrans 'Art and The Travelling Landscape' programme. Look out for *Layering of Time* milestones with poetry along the way, and *The Blockers Seaside* near to Leagrave train station. Both artworks are by artist Isabella Lockett.

Dunstable is a market town at the junction of the ancient roads of Watling Street and Icknield Way, at the foot of the chalk downs. Part of its 12th-century priory survives as the parish church.

The Sewell Greenway provides a delightful escape into nature for walkers, cyclists and horseriders. Built on the old railway line between Stanbridgeford and Frenchs Avenue in Dunstable, the land is a Country Wildlife Site with flora and chalk grassland habitats.

ROUTE INFORMATION

National Route: 6
Start: Luton Airport Parkway station.
Finish: The Green, Stanbridge.
Distance: 10.5 miles (17km).
Grade: Easy, but Sewell Greenway has a long, gentle incline.
Surface: Tarmac roads and rolled sandy surface at the top of Sewell Greenway.
Hills: None.

YOUNG & INEXPERIENCED CYCLISTS

The route is largely traffic-free but includes some road crossings and busy roads, especially in the centre of Luton..

REFRESHMENTS

• Lots of choice in Luton.

Farmland between Ivinghoe and Whipsnade

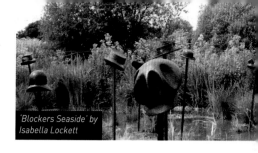
'Blockers Seaside' by
Isabella Lockett

- A number of options in Dunstable, including
  The Globe pub.
- Cafe at Chilterns Gateway Centre.
- The Five Bells pub, Stanbridge.

THINGS TO SEE & DO

- Wardown Park Museum, Luton: galleries in
  landscaped Wardown Park; 01582
  546722;www.wardownparkmuseum.com

- Stockwood Discovery Centre: collections
  exploring the history of the region; 01582
  548600; www.stockwooddiscoverycentre.com
- Chilterns Gateway Centre: off B4541 on the

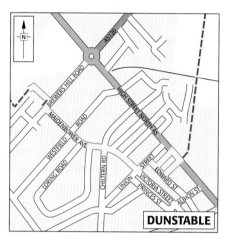

DUNSTABLE

HOUGHTON REGIS

LUTON TO DUNSTABLE & SEWELL GREENWAY

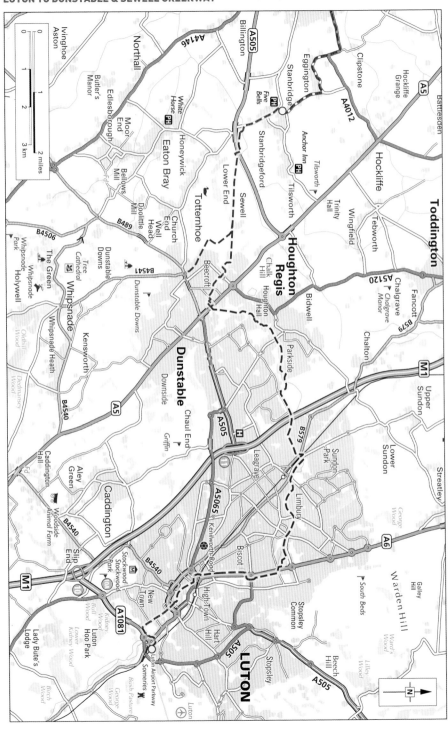

Dunstable Downs; in 500 acres of grassland, with views over the Vale of Aylesbury; perfect for walking, wildlife and flying kites; 01582 500920; www.nationaltrust.org.uk

- **ZSL Whipsnade Zoo:** one of Europe's largest wildlife conservation parks and home to nearly 6,500 animals; www.zsl.org

TRAIN STATIONS
Luton Airport Parkway; Luton; Leagrave.

BIKE HIRE
None locally.

FURTHER INFORMATION
- To view or print National Cycle Network routes, visit www.sustrans.org.uk
- Maps for this area are available to buy from www.sustransshop.co.uk
- **Luton Tourist Information:** 01582 401579; www.luton.gov.uk

ROUTE DESCRIPTION
From Luton Airport Parkway station, follow the road away from the station, then turn right under a subway. Follow the cyclepath to the left, until you join Park Street. Turn right and follow the road to Luton town centre, walking along George Street, then on to New Bedford Road. When you reach the River Lea, the route heads westwards on the new Riverside Way route. Shortly after this point, National Route 6 crosses two major roads on either side of the railway line – please take care here. The route continues traffic-free under the M1 and into Houghton Regis, passing Houghton Hall, then over a stretch of common land along Dog Kennel Path into Dunstable.

National Route 6 continues on roads through the town to the start of the Sewell Greenway, which follows the old branch line between Dunstable and Leighton Buzzard – the Greenway section was said to be the steepest rail incline in the country. The route takes you through an unusually deep cutting between the

Sewell Greenway is a haven for wildlife

chalk downs. To your left as you pass the attractive hamlet of Sewell is the Iron Age hill fort of Maiden Bower. The route crosses the A505 via a new footbridge, and continues to Stanbridgeford, where this section of National Route 6 currently ends, though the Route is signed into the outskirts of Leighton Buzzard.

If you turn south at Sewell, Whipsnade Zoo is under 3 miles (4.8km) away on minor roads.

NEARBY CYCLE ROUTES
When complete, National Route 6 will continue to Leighton Buzzard and Milton Keynes. From there, it is already signposted to Derby.

Between Leighton Buzzard and Linslade, the route joins the towpath and heads north for 6 miles (9.5km) to Bletchley alongside the Grand Union Canal (see page 42). A southerly towpath link from Leighton Buzzard continues to Black Bridge and on to Grove Lock.

From Sewell, a traffic-free path heads south to the southern edge of Dunstable, where a traffic-free route to Dunstable Downs and the Chilterns Gateway Centre is being developed.

An extensive cycle network north of Luton branches off the NCN through Marsh Farm Estate and on to the ancient Great Bramingham Wood (an SSI). It then passes Wauluds Bank, a Mesolithic camp dating to 3000 BC.

LEIGHTON BUZZARD TO BLETCHLEY

Leighton Buzzard is an ancient market town, made attractive by its Georgian high street and market square, which has the twin attractions of a 15th-century market cross and 19th-century former Moot Hall. The Grand Union Canal was first opened from here in the 1920s, when the marriage of numerous small historic waterways created a trunk route from London to Birmingham.

The route goes along a Grand Union Canal towpath which is narrow in places. It is also shared with walkers and anglers, with a 10mph (16km/h) speed limit – ideal for a leisurely cycle ride and for trying to spot a kingfisher. The canal has as its companion the River Ouzel, which meanders away for a while, and then returns, repeating this pattern for the rest of your journey.

Cattle are being reintroduced to the water meadows just north of Leighton Buzzard. This traditional method of husbandry encourages fine grass and meadow flowers, which in turn provide a habitat for a diverse range of wildlife. If you need a break, there is a pub beside the towpath on the northern fringe of Leighton Buzzard at Linslade, and another pub a short distance from the route at Stoke Hammond.

The ride ends at Bletchley, on the southern fringes of Milton Keynes. There is now a museum at Bletchley Park, which played a key role in World War II. It was here that code-breakers worked to decipher the Enigma Code used by German armed forces. There are direct trains from Bletchley back to Leighton Buzzard.

LEIGHTON BUZZARD

BLETCHLEY

ROUTE INFORMATION
National Route: 6
Start: Leighton Buzzard train station.
Finish: Queensway, Bletchley.
Distance: 8 miles (13km).
Grade: Easy.

Surface: Tarmac or fine gravel on the towpath.
Hills: Gentle gradients.

YOUNG & INEXPERIENCED CYCLISTS
Mostly traffic-free with but it does go very close to the canal, so care is needed.

Leighton Buzzard's 15th-c market cross

REFRESHMENTS

- Lots of choice in Leighton Buzzard.
- Some pubs at various points along the towpath, including The Globe Inn.
- Lots of choice in Bletchley.

THINGS TO SEE & DO

- **Leighton Buzzard Railway:** narrow-gauge light railway that offers a 3-mile (5-km), 70-minute round trip from Page's Park to Stonehenge Works, in the Bedfordshire countryside; 01525 373888; www.buzzrail.co.uk

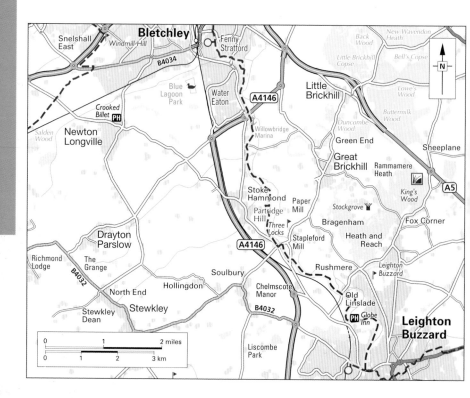

- **Stockgrove Country Park:** 80 acres of parkland, with a lake, ancient woodland, conifer plantations, meadows and heath; 01525 237760; www.greensandtrust.org
- **Blue Lagoon Park:** on the site of a former brickworks; exceptionally clean water and rich in fish and other creatures; includes a Local Nature Reserve; www.milton-keynes.gov.uk
- **Bletchley Park Museum:** historic site of secret British codebreaking activities during World War II and birthplace of the modern computer; 01908 640404; www.bletchleypark.org.uk

TRAIN STATIONS
Leighton Buzzard; Bletchley.

BIKE HIRE
- **Lakeside Cycle Hire, Milton Keynes:** 01908 691616

FURTHER INFORMATION
- To view or print National Cycle Network routes, visit www.sustrans.org.uk
- Maps for this area are available to buy from www.sustransshop.co.uk
- **Leighton Buzzard Tourist Information:** 01525 631920; www.leightonlinslade-tc.gov.uk
- **Buckinghamshire Tourist Information:** 01280 823020; www.visitbuckinghamshire.org

ROUTE DESCRIPTION
From Leighton Buzzard station, turn left onto Station Road, then right onto Old Road. This will bring you out close to a main road junction,

Barge on the Grand Union Canal

Bletchley Park

where there is access to the canal towpath. The 7-mile (11-km) towpath varies in width and has a 10mph (16km/h) speed limit, so take care. This part of the canal has been improved for everybody's benefit, so be considerate to other users and respect any 'dismount' signs.

At Three Locks, you have to use the road, which takes you over the canal, but you are quickly back on the towpath. Soon after you reach Bletchley, you pass under the A4146. Turn onto the bridge at Eaton Lys Farm, then turn right off Mill Street onto Larch Grove. Follow it right round. Dogleg over Manor Road onto Chestnut Crescent and use the traffic-free bridge to access Westfield Road. This will take you to Queensway, the main shopping area in the centre of Bletchley.

NEARBY CYCLE ROUTES

National Route 6 goes north through Milton Keynes as far as Derby, via Northampton and Market Harborough, Leicester and Loughborough. To the south, it passes through Dunstable, Houghton Regis and Luton (see page 38) to Harpenden and eventually London.

National Route 51 runs either side of Milton Keynes and goes as far as Oxford in the west and Sandy in the east (see page 70).

The Milton Keynes redway system is a 120-mile (193-km) network of cycleways and paths for cyclists and pedestrians. It is generally surfaced with red tarmac, and criss-crosses most of the city.

ARLESEY TO LETCHWORTH GARDEN CITY & LETCHWORTH GREENWAY

Arlesey is a little market town with allegedly the longest high street in Britain. There are some interesting walks to be had in the surrounding Bedfordshire countryside, taking you past local rivers, a medieval bridge, lakes and a large country house. There is also a wide range of wildlife to observe.

Built in 1904, Letchworth was the brainchild of Ebenezer Howard, the visionary Victorian social reformer. He believed that the very best of both town and country life should be married together in small 'Garden Cities', each with its own greenbelt. This was the world's first. He promoted well-planned towns with careful land zoning and a high quality of life.

Today, Letchworth has a character all of its own, far from its slightly quirky Arts & Crafts-type origins. The visual effect of Letchworth's planning is seen in the quite impressive approach to its centre along Broadway, with its avenues of linden trees leading to the town square and its attractive rose beds.

The Letchworth Greenway is a 13.5-mile (22-km) circular route that surrounds the Garden City, allowing you to discover the countryside without ever straying far from the town. It truly is 'where town and country meet'.

ROUTE INFORMATION
National Route: 12
Start: Arlesey train station.
Finish: Arlesey train station.
Distance: 16 miles (25.5km).
Grade: Easy.
Surface: Tarmacked roads and lanes.
Hills: one.

YOUNG & INEXPERIENCED CYCLISTS
Mostly traffic-free, with especially easy cycling on the Letchworth Greenway.

REFRESHMENTS
- A number of options in Arlesey, Stotfold and Letchworth.

THINGS TO SEE & DO
- Arlesey Old Moat and Glebe Meadows: riverside walk through meadows and Old Moat nature reserve; plenty of waterside seats and places to picnic; one of eight very pleasant walks around Arlesey; www.arleseywalks.co.uk
- Radwell Meadows: major public recreation facility, with an award-winning children's play area, picnic tables and fixed barbecues.
- Baldock: founded by the Knights Templar in the 12th century but dating back to Roman times, making it one of the county's oldest settlements; well worth a visit.

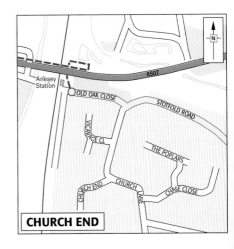

CHURCH END

TRAIN STATIONS
Arlesey; Letchworth Garden City.

BIKE HIRE
None locally.

FURTHER INFORMATION
- To view or print National Cycle Network routes, visit www.sustrans.org.uk
- Maps for this area are available to buy from www.sustransshop.co.uk
- Letchworth Tourist Information: 01462 487868; www.letchworthgc.com
- Garden City Greenway: 01462 476007; www.greenway.org.uk

- **Willian Arboretum:** collection of over 30 different tree varieties; Manor Wood, a few minutes' walk away, has a picnic area.
- **First Garden City Heritage Museum:** housed in a beautiful and unique building, tells the story of the Garden City Movement from its origins to the present day; 01462 482710; www.letchworthgc.com

ROUTE DESCRIPTION
Arlesey station is actually in Church End, so unless you want to go to Arlesey, go straight out of the station onto National Route 12 at Stotfold Road. Where the houses end, you nip left onto the shared path and pass under the A507. Stay on Arlesey Road all the way through Stotfold village. It becomes the High Street and then Baldock Road.

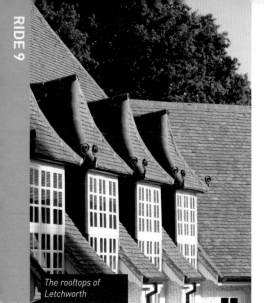

The rooftops of Letchworth

can either ride on Norton Road or cross over to a shared footpath on the opposite side. After just over half a mile (1km) you come to the Letchworth Greenway.

The route goes both ways around the town of Letchworth. Assuming you go left, it takes you through Radwell Meadows Country Park. Go on through Nortonbury. Then ride parallel to the A1, at one point having to cross Norton Road until you get to the railway track, forcing you right. You momentarily go on-road down Blackhorse Road, but left into Knap Close takes you over the railway track onto the greenway. Turn left under the A1(M), then cross Letchworth Road at the traffic lights into Weston Way. You will have to join the carriageway for a short distance at the fire station before turning right to rejoin the Greenway. You are briefly back on road down

Fork right into Murrell Road, then right (south) into Norton Road, where the route leads to an underpass. After crossing the A507, you

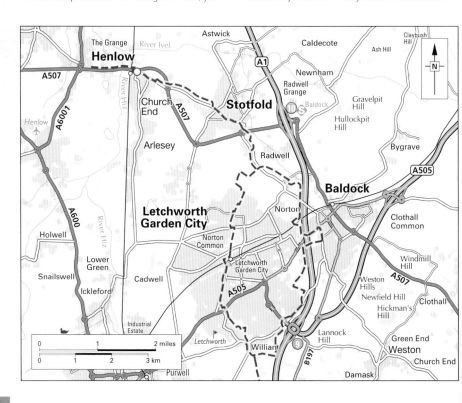

Letchworth Heritage Museum

Radburn Way just before the Letchworth Gate, which once you cross over takes you into Willian Village.

To go back through Letchworth, follow the signs into town. You will get on-road again when you cross the Baldock Road (A505). Spring Road will take you to a roundabout, then onto Broadway to the town centre. Turn left past the station, go over the bridge, take the first right, then left, and cross Icknield Way onto Norton Common. Back on-road through the Grange Estate, then the cyclepath to rejoin the Norton/Stotfold road.

To avoid the town centre, take the Letchworth Greenway all the way round the outskirts, past the golf course and eventually past the Standalone Farm. However, this is not a continuous route for cyclists.

Buildings in Baldock town centre

NEARBY CYCLE ROUTES

The 32-mile (51.5-km) long Great North Way takes you from Letchworth to Potters Bar, via Hatfield, on National Route 12.

FLITCH WAY – BRAINTREE TO LITTLE DUNMOW

Braintree is at the junction of Roman roads running from Chelmsford and Colchester. By the 19th century, the town had become a thriving industrial centre, partly thanks to the coming of the railway. The Braintree to Bishop's Stortford line, decommissioned in 1972, now enjoys a new lease of life as a country park full of railway cuttings rich in wildlife and dotted with attractive Victorian stations.

The first of these on this route is Rayne station, now a visitor centre with an exhibition about the old railway. There are many public footpaths exploring the local countryside just off the Flitch Way, and a Wildside Walk pack is available from the Rayne Station Centre.

The story behind the name of the route lies in the village of Little Dunmow. In a rare example of a folk custom surviving today, the Flitch Trial is held every four years and requires a married couple to stand before a mock court. If they can prove to the satisfaction of the judge and jury that they have, for a year and a day, 'not wished themselves unwed', then they are awarded half a pig, known as a flitch (a side) of bacon. Although the custom originated in Little Dunmow, the modern trial is held in Great Dunmow.

Dunmow Priory is reputed to be the last resting place of Maid Marian. Legend has it that she went there to live with the nuns after the death of Robin Hood, and was killed by a poisoned bracelet sent by King John in an act of belated revenge. All that remains of the Priory now is its church at Little Dunmow.

Bringing home the bacon at the Flitch Trial

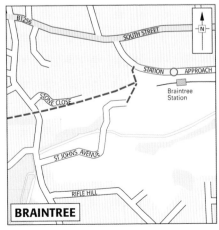

BRAINTREE

Varied house fronts
at Great Dunmow

ROUTE INFORMATION
National Route: 16
Start: Braintree train station.
Finish: The Street, Little Dunmow (Flitch of Bacon pub).
Distance: 8 miles (13km).
Grade: Easy.
Surface: Good stone-based track.
Hills: None.

Braintree District
Museum

YOUNG & INEXPERIENCED CYCLISTS
The route follows an old railway track and therefore is mainly traffic-free, except for an on-road section to the Flitch of Bacon pub.

REFRESHMENTS
- Lots of choice in Braintree.
- Cafe at Rayne station (weekends only).
- Welsh Princess pub, Rayne.
- Flitch of Bacon pub, Little Dunmow.

THINGS TO SEE & DO
- **Braintree District Museum:** award-winning museum in converted school tells the fascinating story of a little-known artistic and industrial heritage; gallery, cafe, craft and gift shop; 01376 325266; www.enjoybraintreedistrict.co.uk

- **Rayne Station Centre:** visitor centre with an exhibition about the old railway, and a cafe at weekends; 01736 340262
- **Great Notley Country Park Discovery Centre:** south of Braintree; beautiful walks around lakes, meadows and woods, set in a 100-acre country park; www.greatnotley.com

TRAIN STATIONS
Braintree.

BIKE HIRE
- Cycle Centre, Great Notley Country Park: 01376 348275; www.trailnet.org.uk

FURTHER INFORMATION
- To view or print National Cycle Network routes, visit www.sustrans.org.uk

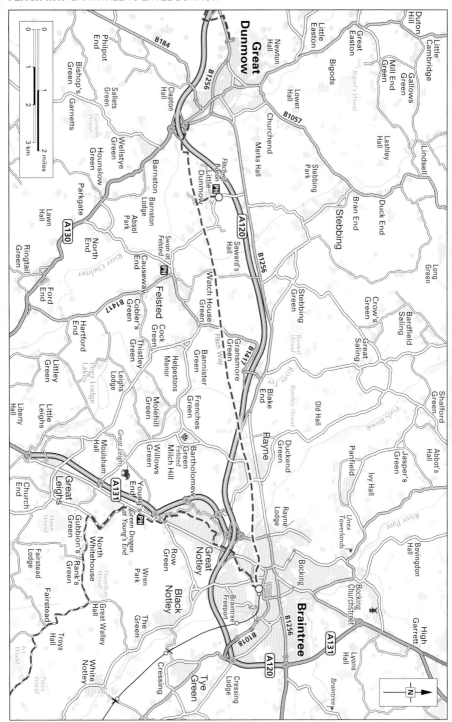

- Maps for this area are available to buy from
  www.sustransshop.co.uk
- Braintree Tourist Information: 01376 550066;
  www.enjoybraintree.co.uk
- Friends of the Flitch Way:
  www.friends-of-the-flitch-way.org.uk

ROUTE DESCRIPTION

Turn left out of Braintree station and go to the
end of the long-stay car park furthest from the
station. The ride is traffic-free for 8 miles
(13km) as you follow the old railway line. Little
Dunmow is the turnaround point of the ride, as
the Flitch Way ends just west of the village and
there is currently no completed route through
Great Dunmow. In order to get to the Flitch of
Bacon pub, you have to leave the railway track
at Little Dunmow, descend to the road, turn

right and proceed along the road for just short
of a mile (1.6km).

NEARBY CYCLE ROUTES

National Route 16 continues beyond Little
Dunmow, so if you wish to extend the ride and
your party is equal to busy main roads, you can
make your way through Great Dunmow and
pick up the Flitch Way again about a mile
(1.6km) west of the town along the B1256. From
there it heads along the edge of Hatfield Forest
to Tilekiln Green, just east of Bishop's Stortford
and the M11. There are plans to create a
continuous route through Great Dunmow, and
to connect the Flitch Way to a new link to
Stansted Airport.

COLCHESTER TO HADLEIGH

Colchester is Britain's oldest recorded town, with a colourful history dating back over 2,000 years. The earliest record of Colchester's existence is a reference by the Roman writer Pliny the Elder in AD 77. In addition, Colchester Castle was the first royal castle outside of London, and pre-dates the Tower of London; in fact, it was the blueprint for it.

Colchester has plenty of open spaces and nature reserves. Largest of these is High Woods Country Park on the north of the town. The Visitor Centre, which is open at weekends, is the place to find out all about the natural history of this ancient piece of landscape.

This route is in the heart of 'Constable Country', and the town of Dedham is part of the Painter's Trail. Once a Viking Royal Town, Hadleigh has a 15th-century guildhall and fine Georgian and medieval buildings. It is the reputed resting place of Danish King Guthrum, said to be buried in the grounds of St Mary Church. The Hadleigh Railway Walk is worth a jaunt. It is only 2 miles (3km) long and runs from Station Road to the outskirts of Raydon village. The walk follows the route of the old railway line and takes in the new suburbs and views of the old halls in the town's hinterland. Notable features on the route are the old stations, the Sustrans Milepost Sculpture and the Hunters Bridge in the section that cuts through Raydon Great Wood. The Milepost Sculpture is one of a thousand mileposts of various designs, funded by the Royal Bank of Scotland.

ROUTE INFORMATION
National Route: 1
Start: Colchester train station.
Finish: Duke Street, Hadleigh.
Distance: 15 miles (24km).
Grade: Easy.
Surface: Tarmac and fine gravel paths.
Hills: Gently, rolling hills.

YOUNG & INEXPERIENCED CYCLISTS
Mainly quiet roads with some pleasant traffic-free sections. Although most of the country roads are quiet, the traffic on some of them is very fast, so care is needed on this route.

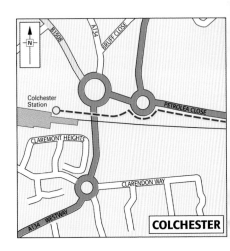

REFRESHMENTS
- Lots of choice in Colchester.
- The Sun Inn, Dedham, just off the route.
- Three fine pubs in Stratford St Mary.
- A number of options in Hadleigh.

THINGS TO SEE & DO
- Colchester Castle Museum: largest keep ever built by the Normans, constructed on the foundations of the Roman Temple of Claudius; spectacular hands-on displays of the town's history, from the Stone Age to the English Civil War; 01206 282939;

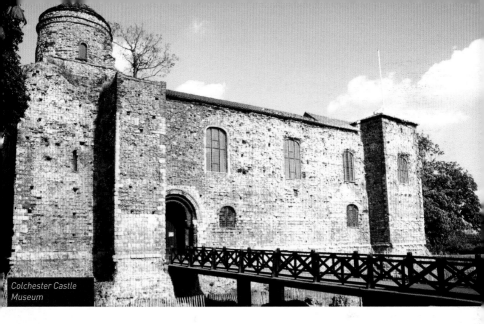

Colchester Castle Museum

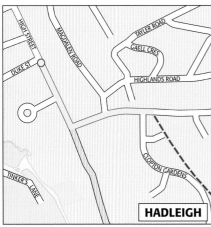

HADLEIGH

www.colchestermuseums.org.uk
- **Hollytrees Museum:** elegant Georgian town house built in 1718, with collections from the 18th to 20th century; 01206 282940; www.colchestermuseums.org.uk
- **High Woods Country Park:** 330 acres of woodland, grassland and wetland with a path network, including a 3-mile (5-km) circular walk and easy access trail; 01206 853588; www.visitcolchester.com
- **The Fuzz:** Nature Reserve on the southeast edge of Hadleigh; connected to the Hadleigh Railway Walk and a public right of way.

- **Wolves Wood:** east of Hadleigh; RSPB reserve and one of the few remnants of the ancient woodland that used to cover East Anglia; 01473 328006; www.rspb.org.uk

TRAIN STATIONS
Colchester.

BIKE HIRE
- **Bike Hire Colchester:** 01206 521312; www.bikehirecolchester.co.uk
- **Pedal Partners, Colchester:** 01621 815690

FURTHER INFORMATION
- To view or print National Cycle Network routes, visit www.sustrans.org.uk
- Maps for this area are available to buy from www.sustransshop.co.uk
- **Colchester Tourist Information:** 01206 282920; www.visitcolchester.com

ROUTE DESCRIPTION
Turn right out of the main exit at Colchester train station and head for the foot/cycle bridge that goes from near the station entrance over the busy A134. Follow the signed traffic-free route along Petrolea Close to High Woods Country Park. Cycle on down the path until it hits National Route 1.

Boats on the River Stour at Dedham

Alternatively, turn left out of the station, taking care at the roundabout. Turn left again, go up Bruff Close, continue straight over, then go down Turner Road and right down Brickmakers Lane into High Woods Country Park.

Except for a couple of brief stretches, the route is traffic-free until just before you leave Colchester and go over the A12 on Severalls Lane. Follow the signposted National Route 1 through Dedham Vale and some attractive villages, particularly Stratford St Mary. It has three coaching inns to choose from should you require a little stopping-off point. After the village of Raydon, the route becomes traffic-free through Raydon Great Wood as you go along the 2-mile (3-km) long Hadleigh Railway

Walk. It follows a disused railway line, which takes you to Station Road in Hadleigh. Turn left, then second right into High Street to reach Duke Street.

As an alternative, just before Raydon near the village of Holton St Mary, follow an on-road route east (National Route 1), via Lower Raydon and Shelley, and then go north to Hadleigh.

NEARBY CYCLE ROUTES

Northwards, National Route 1 leaves Hadleigh on the Hadleigh Railway Walk then heads through Ipswich forming part of the Fakenham to Harwich cycle route.

National Route 51 goes from Colchester to Harwich (see page 58), and on to Newmarket, via Ipswich and Bury St Edmunds.

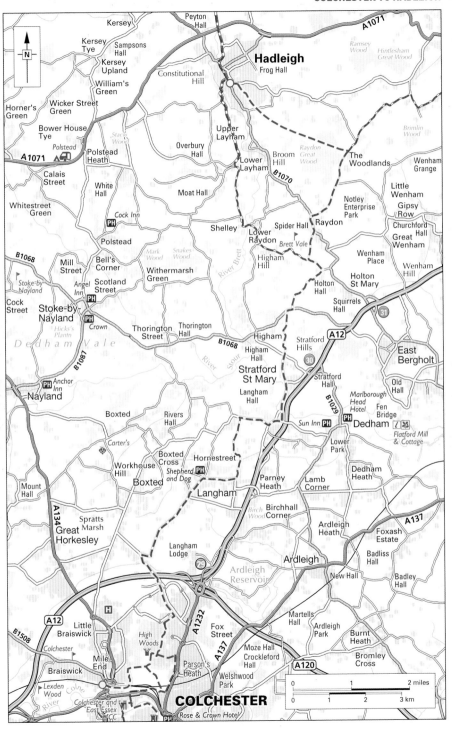

HARWICH TO WIVENHOE & COLCHESTER

Harwich has a rich maritime history and is highly regarded for its architectural heritage. Most of the older part of the town is a conservation area and it boasts the oldest unaltered purpose-built cinema in Britain, the Electric Palace Cinema, opened in 1911.

This route takes you from the Blue Flag beach coast through some of the loveliest Essex countryside and on to the Wivenhoe Trail to historic Colchester. As the oldest recorded town in Britain, Colchester is alive with history and culture, with much to offer visitors. The area has inspired artists such as John Constable and Thomas Gainsborough, and there are wonderful examples of buildings and architecture from Roman times to the present day, including Colchester Castle and Museum.

Colchester is also a great starting point for exploring the surrounding countryside by bike because of the pleasant country lanes, its proximity to several coastal towns that burst with character and charm, and the convenient location of many easily accessible train stations.

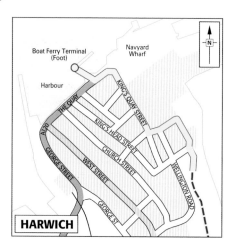

ROUTE INFORMATION
National Route: 51
Start: Ha'penny pier for Harwich foot ferry.
Finish: High Street, Colchester.
Distance: 24 miles (38.5km).
Grade: Easy.
Surface: Tarmac and fine gravel paths.
Hills: Gently rolling, no challenging gradients.

YOUNG & INEXPERIENCED CYCLISTS
Some pleasant traffic-free sections but some busy roads too. Take care on the short section along the A133.

REFRESHMENTS
- Lots of choice in Harwich, including the New Bell Inn, Samuel Pepys pub and The Ha'penny Pier cafe.
- A number of options in Wivenhoe.
- Lots of choice in Colchester.

THINGS TO SEE & DO
Harwich:
- **Maritime Museum:** housed in a disused lighthouse; 01255 552488; www.harwich-society.co.uk
- **Harwich Redoubt Fort:** circular fort

Harwich docks seen from Shotley Gate

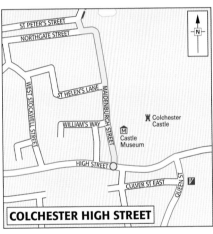

COLCHESTER HIGH STREET

(map labels: ST PETER'S STREET, NORTHGATE STREET, WEST STOCKWELL STREET, ST HELEN'S LANE, MAIDENBURGH STREET, WILLIAM'S WAY, HIGH STREET, CULVER ST EAST, QUEEN ST, Colchester Castle, Castle Museum)

Colchester:
- **Colchester Castle Museum:** Norman castle housing an award-winning museum; www.colchestermuseums.org.uk
- **Hollytrees Museum:** beautiful Georgian town house built in 1718 and now an award-winning museum; 01206 282940; www.colchestermuseums.org.uk

TRAIN STATIONS
Harwich Town; Wivenhoe; Hythe; Colchester.

BIKE HIRE
- **Bike Hire Colchester:** 01206 521312; www.bikehirecolchester.co.uk

FURTHER INFORMATION
- To view or print National Cycle Network routes, visit www.sustrans.org.uk
- Maps for this area are available to buy from www.sustransshop.co.uk
- **Harwich Tourist Information:** 01255 506139; www.harwich.net
- **Colchester Tourist Information:** 01206 282920; www.visitcolchester.com

commanding the harbour built during the Napoleonic Wars; 01255 503429; www.harwich-society.co.uk
- **RSPB Stour Estuary Nature Reserve:** one of the most important estuaries in Britain for wintering birds; masses of wading birds and wildfowl at Copperas Bay; nature trails and picnic areas. 01473 328006; www.rspb.org.uk
- **Wivenhoe:** former fishing and boat-building community, with picturesque quayside and Saxon church; adjacent to Wivenhoe Woods, an ancient 40-acre sweet chestnut woodland; www.wivenhoe.gov.uk

ROUTE DESCRIPTION
Harwich Harbour separates Harwich on the Essex side of the Stour estuary from Shotley

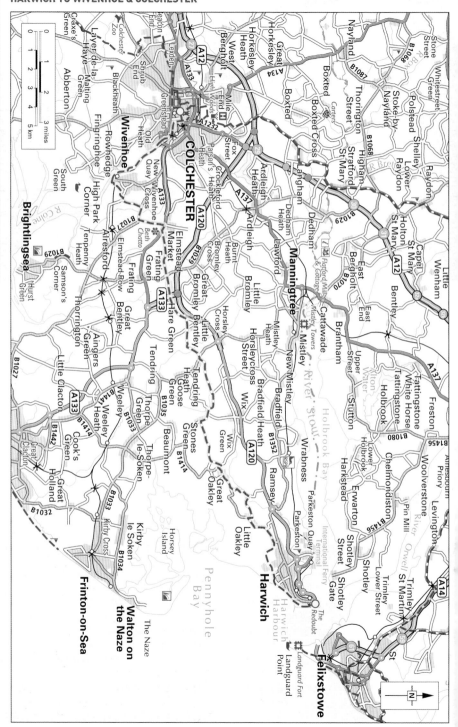

and Felixstowe on the Suffolk side. The foot and cycle ferry departs from Ha'penny Pier on Parkeston Quay in Harwich, where this route begins. Take the shared-use seafront path and enjoy the views of the beach as you do so. The small iron lighthouses, or 'Leading Lights', that sit along the front are a notable feature. Follow signs for National Route 51 past the Blue Flag beach and out of Dovercourt, to leave the buildings behind. There follows 10 miles (16km) of magnificent cycling on level, tranquil lanes through Little Oakley, Great Oakley and Tendring Heath, with delightful vistas and attractive villages.

There are shops and a small village green at Elmstead Market if you need to stop for refreshments but take care as you go briefly along the A133. Turn left towards Elmstead Heath. Be careful along the B1027 at Keelers Tye as well. Turn onto Tye Lane towards Wivenhoe and follow the route down to the Quay, which runs alongside the River Colne close to the quayside, to enjoy the views and perhaps the refreshments from the riverside pub. This is where the traffic-free and

family-friendly Wivenhoe Trail begins, taking you by the river, with green parkland and fields on either side, until you reach Colchester.

Follow the route alongside the river, crossing the river twice before the route takes you into Colchester town centre, continuing along streets with Castle Park on you left, until you reach the High Street.

NEARBY CYCLE ROUTES
The Harwich Harbour Foot Ferry runs throughout the summer, taking foot passengers and their bicycles to Shotley or Felixstowe, where you can continue on Route 51 to Ipswich, for a train back to Colchester. Alternatively, you can ride through Felixstowe to Felixstowe Ferry, which takes you on to the Suffolk Coastal Route (see page 62). This joins up with National Route 1, which, again, could take you back to Colchester. If that's not far enough, take the North Sea Cycle Route from Dovercourt to Harwich International Port. There you can catch the ferry to continue the route in Denmark or the Netherlands!

Low tide at Wivenhoe

FELIXSTOWE TO ORFORD

Felixstowe has a rich military past and a unique place in English history – it was the last place a foreign force invaded the land. In July 1667, 2,000 Dutch soldiers came ashore, but the garrison at Landguard Fort successfully repelled the attackers. By 1720, the fort had been replaced with a new one, and Daniel Defoe then hailed it as 'one of the best and securest in England'. Landguard Fort still stands today and, even though the soldiers may have left, it is open to the public.

Felixstowe became a major port in 1886, and today it is an attractive Victorian seaside town. Known as the 'Sun Spot of the East Coast', it features in the *Good Beach Guide*. The pier constructed in 1905 is now unsafe. The route from Felixstowe to Landguard Fort is being improved by a new traffic-free section.

Orford became a thriving commercial and fishing seaport until the growth of Orford Ness cut it off from the sea and access was redirected through the mouth of the River Ore. The church and the quay were built by the Normans, and Orford grew in importance in the 12th century when Henry II commissioned a castle to be built.

This route is a beautiful one along the Suffolk coastline but it does rely on two ferries. Crossings may be possible only at certain times of the year so please check in advance.

ROUTE INFORMATION

National Route: 51 **Regional Route:** 41
Start: Felixstowe train station.
Finish: Orford Castle.
Distance: 16 miles (25.5km).
Grade: Medium; bikes must be carried onto ferries, including over a stile.
Surface: Tarmac and fine gravel paths.
Hills: Some short, steep hills.

YOUNG & INEXPERIENCED CYCLISTS

Not really suitable.

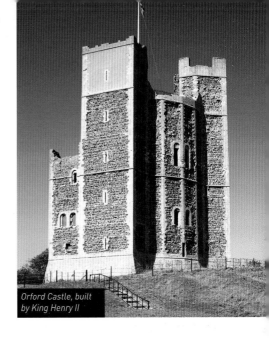

REFRESHMENTS
- Lots of choice in Felixstowe.
- The Ferry Boat Inn and Victoria pub, Felixstowe Ferry.
- Some options in Orford, including the Kings Head pub.

THINGS TO SEE & DO
- **Felixstowe Museum:** 14 rooms of artefacts, displaying the military and social history of Felixstowe; 01394 674355; www.felixstowe-museum.co.uk
- **Landguard Fort:** guided tours and nature reserve; open April to November; 07749 695523; www.landguard.com
- **Orford Castle:** medieval castle with three towers and a maze of rooms and passageways to explore; 01394 450472; www.english-heritage.org.uk
- **Orford Ness National Nature Reserve:** wild and remote extremity of eastern England with the largest vegetated shingle spit in Europe; internationally important flora and fauna; 01394 450901; www.nationaltrust.org.uk

Orford Castle, built by King Henry II

TRAIN STATIONS
Felixstowe.

FERRIES
- **Bawdsey Ferry:** for foot passengers and cyclists, across the River Deben between Felixstowe Ferry and Bawdsey; seasonal service; 01394 282173
- **Butley Ferry:** for foot passengers and cyclists (no tandems) from Easter to September; operated by volunteers at weekends and bank holidays in summer; can be prebooked;

Orford Ness

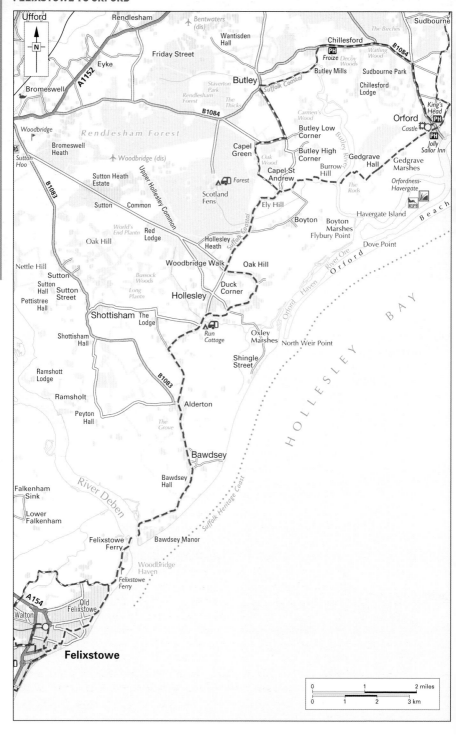

Colourful beach huts at Felixstowe

01394 450843; www.aldeandore.org

BIKE HIRE

- Alford Bros, Felixstowe: 01394 284719;
  www.alfordbrothers.co.uk

FURTHER INFORMATION

- To view or print National Cycle Network
  routes, visit www.sustrans.org.uk
- Maps for this area are available to buy from
  www.sustransshop.co.uk
- Felixstowe Tourist Information:
  01394 276770; www.visitfelixstowe.co.uk

ROUTE DESCRIPTION

You have to follow a slightly complicated route towards Felixstowe Ferry but, essentially, you are heading east. From Felixstowe station, head through the old station building (you will need to walk), which will take you to Hamilton Road. Go down Hamilton Road (past Alford Brothers). This connects to National Route 51, where you cross Cobbold Road. Continue down Hamilton Road and turn left at Hamilton Gardens (don't go down Bent Hill). Follow Hamilton Gardens and Cambridge Road, then turn right into Cobbold Road. Go down Bath Hill and along Undercliff Road East, leading to Maybush Lane. Turn right into Golf Road. Turn

right at Cliff Road and follow it to Felixstowe Ferry. It becomes Regional Route 41 at Felixstowe Ferry Golf Club.

Take the Bawdsey Ferry – check in advance that it is running – across the River Deben. On the other side, follow the Ferry Road left and round through Bawdsey to Alderton. The road is well signposted, with some lovely sea views. When you get to Capel St Andrew, follow the signs to Butley Ferry. Access to the ferry is along a steep footpath and over a stile – again, check in advance that it is running. (A route avoiding the ferry is signed the Suffolk Coast Route with Regional Route 41 patches.)

Once over the water, you pass through Gedgrave Estate and find your way to Orford.

NEARBY CYCLE ROUTES

Regional Route 41 (The Suffolk Coastal Cycle) combines with National Route 1 to form an 88-mile (142-km) circular route north of Felixstowe through Orford, Blaxhall and Bruisyard. There it joins Route 1 to Woodbridge and returns to Felixstowe via Waldringfield.

The North Sea Cycle Route is a 3,730-mile (6,000-km) long-distance route that encircles the countries bordering the North Sea, and uses many international ferry links.

IPSWICH TO WOODBRIDGE

Ipswich is England's oldest continuously settled Anglo-Saxon town, with impressive medieval streets and quite a few architectural gems, from the decorative plasterwork of the Ancient House (c.1670) to Sir Norman Foster's award-winning Willis Corroon building, the first building of the 1970s to be listed. It also boasts 12 medieval churches, a Victorian wet dock and a fine Tudor mansion. Christchurch Mansion houses a collection of pottery and glass, a contemporary art gallery and a notable collection of paintings by artists including John Constable and Thomas Gainsborough. The house is surrounded by Christchurch Park, a grand 70-acre landscaped park featuring many beautiful trees, rolling lawns and a duck pond.

At the other end of the route is the charming town of Woodbridge. This is overlooked by Sutton Hoo, a group of low grassy mounds. It is the burial ground of Anglo-Saxon kings of East Anglia, where priceless treasure was discovered in a 27.5-m (90-ft) long ship grave. The town is also adjacent to Rendlesham Forest, famous for an incident in 1980 when an extraterrestrial spaceship supposedly landed. So if you decide to picnic there, check your neighbours carefully!

ROUTE INFORMATION
National Route: 1
Start: Ipswich train station.
Finish: Woodbridge train station.
Distance: 11 miles (17.5km).
Grade: Easy to moderate.
Surface: Tarmac or fine gravel paths.
Hills: Short and steep.

YOUNG & INEXPERIENCED CYCLISTS
Mostly on-road sections. Traffic-free through Grange Farm, Kesgrave.

REFRESHMENTS
- Lots of choice in Ipswich, Kesgrave and Martlesham.
- Lots of choice in Woodbridge, including the Waterfront Cafe, Tide Mill Way.

Inside Christchurch Mansion

THINGS TO SEE & DO
Ipswich:
- **Ipswich Museum:** founded in 1847; stunning Victorian natural history gallery; also charts the development of the town from the beginnings of life on the River Orwell during the Ice Age through to the present day; 01473 433550; www.ipswich.gov.uk
- **Christchurch Mansion:** fine Tudor building set in an ancient and beautiful park with historic room settings; outstanding paintings and furniture; 01473 433554; www.ipswich.gov.uk
- **Orwell Country Park:** 200-acre site south of the town, offering a variety of walks, wildlife and scenery; stunning views over the river estuary; 01473 433993; www.ipswich.gov.uk
- **Martlesham Heath:** control tower and museum, crammed full of interesting paraphernalia, giving the history of the historic airfield; restricted opening; www.mhas.org.uk

Woodbridge:
- **Woodbridge Museum:** small, friendly museum with exhibits reflecting the history of Woodbridge and its townspeople; 01394 380502; www.visitwoodbridge.co.uk

The Ancient House at Ipswich

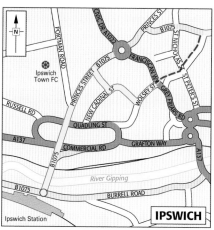

IPSWICH

WOODBRIDGE

- **Shire Hall:** iconic focal point of the town for over 400 years; 01394 383599; www.visitwoodbridge.co.uk
- **Suffolk Horse Museum:** award-winning museum devoted to the Suffolk punch breed of heavy working horse; 01394 380643; www.suffolkhorsesociety.org.uk
- **Woodbridge Tide Mill:** built in the 18th century and the last working tide mill in the UK; 01473 384880; www.woodbridgesuffolk.info
- **Sutton Hoo:** burial ground of the Anglo-Saxon kings of East Anglia, overlooking river;

01394 389700; www.nationaltrust.org.uk; www.suttonhoo.org
- **Rendlesham Forest:** 3,707 acres of coniferous plantations as well as broadleaved belts, heathland and wetland areas; www.forestry.gov.uk

TRAIN STATIONS

Ipswich; Woodbridge.

BIKE HIRE

- **Bicycle Doctor & Hire Service, Ipswich:** 01473 259853; www.bicycledoctor.gbr.fm

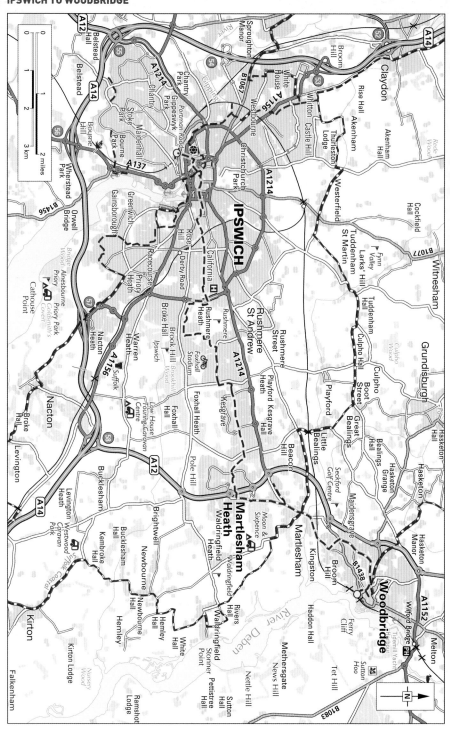

Woodbridge Tide Mill

FURTHER INFORMATION

- To view or print National Cycle Network routes, visit www.sustrans.org.uk
- Maps for this area are available to buy from www.sustransshop.co.uk
- Ipswich Tourist Information: 01473 258070; www.visit-ipswich.com
- Woodbridge Tourist Information: 01394 382240; www.suffolkcoastal.gov.uk

ROUTE DESCRIPTION

Straight out of Ipswich station, proceed over the river bridge into Princes Street. Go right into the bus lane or use the cyclepath on the left. Cross two sets of traffic lights and turn right into Chalon Street (there's a toucan crossing before the turn). Turn left into New Cardinal Street and follow Cecilia Street, bearing left into Wolsey Street. Go straight over at the traffic lights onto the Cutler Street cyclepath. Turn left and then right into Silent Street. Go right again at the mini roundabout into Old Cattle Market, leading to Dog's Head Street.

Follow signposted National Route 1 out of town. At the end of Newbury Road, the cyclepath continues down the right of Ipswich Hospital, enabling you to come out in Heath Road. Turn left to use the toucan crossing and turn right to pass Rushmere Heath. Turn left

into Gleneagles Drive, following residential roads around the edge of Rushmere Heath, before turning right onto Penzance Road.

At the end of Penzance Road, turn left into Bell Lane. A little further along, turn right into Twelve Acre Approach, where you will shortly enter the traffic-free section through Grange Farm Kesgrave. Kesgrave High School has one of the highest level of cycling students in the country, comparable with the best on the Continent. Cross the A12 over the shared-use footbridge and then turn left towards Woodbridge, following roads all the way into the town. At the end of the Thoroughfare in Woodbridge, ignore the right-turn sign for Route 1. Instead, turn left into Quay Street, then right into Station Road.

NEARBY CYCLE ROUTES

National Route 1 follows the Fakenham to Harwich cycle route north, passing through Norwich, King's Lynn and Lincoln. To the south, National Route 1 travels from Ipswich through Suffolk to Colchester, Essex.

National Route 51 goes west from Ipswich to Bury St Edmunds and Newmarket, and all the way to Oxford via Cambridge, Bedford and Milton Keynes. To the south, it travels from Ipswich to Felixstowe, Harwich and Wivenhoe.

BEDFORD TO SANDY

Bedford has been a market town for the surrounding agricultural area for many centuries. Two castles were built in Norman times but were destroyed in 1224, with only a mound remaining today. Bedford's most famous son is John Bunyan, the author of *The Pilgrim's Progress*, who was imprisoned for his beliefs for 12 years in Bedford Gaol in the late 17th century. Built in 1849, the Meeting House is located on the original site of the barn where he preached, and the nearby Bunyan Museum contains personal relics. An interesting fact about Bedford is that it has one of the highest concentrations of Italian immigrants in the UK – almost 30% of the population is Italian or of Italian descent. Perhaps not surprisingly, Bedford's Little Italy has an impressive variety of Italian bars, restaurants and delicatessens.

Sandy's history dates back to Roman times: Caesar's Camp is an ancient hill fort set in the wooded hills to the southeast of the town. Nowadays, Sandy is more famous as the headquarters of the Royal Society for the Protection of Birds (RSPB), which is adjacent to The Lodge nature reserve, a mixture of formal gardens with large specimen trees and an azalea walk, heathland and woodland, giving visitors the opportunity of seeing some 100 species of birds.

ROUTE INFORMATION

National Routes: 51 and 12
Start: Bedford Embankment by the town bridge.
Finish: Sandy market place.

Distance: 9 miles (14.5km).
Grade: Easy.
Surface: Smooth and level route, mainly following riverside paths or a disused railway.
Hills: None.

Bedford's Butterfly Bridge

Willington dovecote and stables

YOUNG & INEXPERIENCED CYCLISTS

Nearly all traffic-free. Mainly quiet roads in Sandy.

REFRESHMENTS

- Lots of choice in Bedford.
- Priory Country Park.
- Visitor Centre at Danish Camp, Willington.
- Sandy market place.

THINGS TO SEE & DO

- Bedford Victorian Embankment Gardens.
- John Bunyan Museum, Bedford: 01234 213722; www.bedfordmuseum.org/ johnbunyanmuseum
- **Priory Country Park:** a haven for wildlife, with lakes, meadows, woodland and a visitor centre; 01234 211182; www.priorycountrypark.co.uk
- **Willington Dovecote and Stables:** 16th-century stable and stone dovecote now in the care of the National Trust; viewing by appointment with the volunteer custodian on 01234 838278; www.nationaltrust.org.uk
- **Danish Camp, Willington:** historic monument, where the Vikings are believed to have repaired their boats; visitor centre, refreshments, day fishing and boat rides on the river; 01234 838709; www.danishcamp.co.uk
- **Blunham:** a pretty village dating back to Saxon times.

A Green Woodpecker

BEDFORD TO SANDY

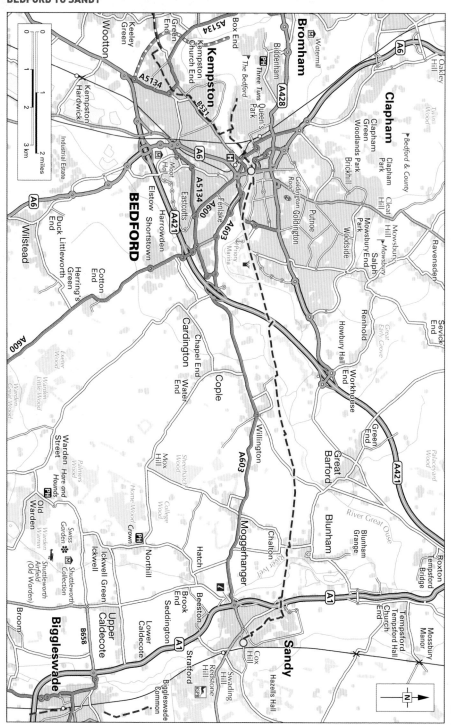

- **Sandy:** market gardening centre since the early 17th century.
- **The Lodge nature reserve (RSPB), Sandy:** beautiful gardens with opportunities to spot woodpeckers and other woodland birds; 01767 680551; www.rspb.org.uk

TRAIN STATIONS
Bedford; Sandy.

BIKE HIRE
- Marina Cycles, Priory Country Park: 01234 340090
- Danish Camp, Willington: 01234 838709; www.danishcamp.co.uk

FURTHER INFORMATION
- To view or print National Cycle Network routes, visit www.sustrans.org.uk
- Maps for this area are available to buy from www.sustransshop.co.uk
- Bedford Tourist Information: 01234 221712; www.bedford.gov.uk/tourism

ROUTE DESCRIPTION
Beginning in the centre of Bedford by the Town Bridge, follow the embankment past the castle mound to the elegant Victorian Embankment Gardens. Follow the River Ouse Newcut to the wildlife haven of Priory Country Park. The ride then continues along the route of a former railway, crossing the A421 and passing Willington Dovecote. The route rejoins the river for a while, bringing you to the Danish Camp. From there, you ride through the pretty village of Blunham, following Station Court, turning south on to Station Road and east again to rejoin the railway line. Cross over the River Ivel and cycle into Sandy, going under the A1 before joining paths and quiet roads that lead to the centre of Sandy, where the bustling market place is a focal point. The Lodge nature reserve (home to the RSPB) is on the southeastern side of the town, and is well worth a visit.

Statue of John Bunyan in Bedford

OTHER NEARBY CYCLE ROUTES
National Route 12 heads north–south from Peterborough to beyond Hatfield, merging with Route 51 in the Sandy area. Route 12 is only partly completed, but the intention is for it to continue through St Neots and Biggleswade. There are plans for an orbital route around Bedford, which will be known as The Bedford Green Wheel. Route 51 continues along the River Great Ouse, west from Bedford town centre through Kempston before following minor roads to the Forest Centre and Millennium Country Park at Marston Moretaine. This is a popular area for cycling and away from busy roads. There are many attractive quiet lanes and villages popular with cyclists in Bedfordshire, including The Thatcher's Way, which starts at Priory Country Park.

CAMBRIDGE TO ANGLESEY ABBEY

Cambridge is already a cycling city. In 2008, it was awarded National Cycling Town status, which will see £7.2 million spent on cycling improvements in Cambridge and surrounding villages before March 2011. It is also very much a university city, with many colleges open to visitors, although not during the exam revision season from mid-April to mid-June.

Although this is an urban route in daily use by local cyclists, it is particularly verdant, leaving the city from Jesus Green, via Midsummer Common, Stourbridge Common and Ditton Meadows. (If you want to start the ride at the station, a complicated but well-signposted route is available.) The route follows the River Cam through the city. You may see punts on the river at the very beginning of the route, but thereafter the river usually belongs to rowing teams.

You pass by the Museum of Technology in the old Pumping Station, which is well worth a visit. When you leave the river, you pass the airfield and the pretty village of Stow-cum-Quy, where the church dates back to 1340. Bottisham is another attractive village. While there, it's worth carrying on a little further to Anglesey Abbey, a Jacobean house owned by the National Trust. In the gardens, there is a water mill, which operates on the first and third Saturday of each month, subject to water levels.

ROUTE INFORMATION

National Route: 51
Start: Jesus Green, Cambridge.
Finish: Anglesey Abbey, Lode.
Distance: 8 miles (13km).

Grade: Easy.
Surface: Flat and mostly traffic-free, with a couple of short on-road sections.
Hills: None.

Gatehouse, St John's College, Cambridge

Mathematical Bridge over the River Cam

YOUNG & INEXPERIENCED CYCLISTS

Flat and mostly traffic-free, with a couple of short on-road sections. Particular care is needed in Cambridge city centre, however, which is often very busy. There is a busy road to cross near Anglesey Abbey.

REFRESHMENTS

- Lots of choice in Cambridge.

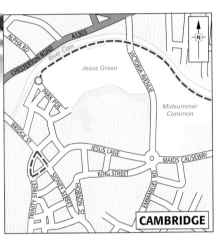

- Pubs in Stow-cum-Quy and Bottisham.
- Restaurant at Anglesey Abbey.

THINGS TO SEE & DO

- University colleges; www.cam.ac.uk
- **Fitzwilliam Museum:** the collection includes paintings from the 14th century, sculpture, oriental art and antiquities from Egypt, the Ancient Near East, Greece, Rome and Cyprus; 01223 332900; www.fitzmuseum.cam.ac.uk
- **Cambridge Museum of Technology:** based in the original sewage pumping station for Cambridge; exhibits include the pumping station's original equipment and other engines; 01223 368650 www.visitcambridge.org
- **Anglesey Abbey:** famously eclectic collection of paintings and furniture; 18th-century working water mill in the gardens, which are of interest year round; National Trust shop, plant centre, fully licensed restaurant; closed Mondays and Tuesdays; 01223 810080; www.angleseyabbey.org

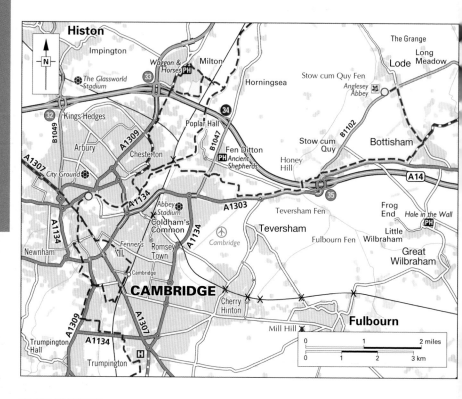

TRAIN STATIONS
Cambridge.

BIKE HIRE
- City Cycle Hire, Cambridge: 01223 365629; www.citycyclehire.com
- Cambridge Station Cycles: 01223 307125; www.stationcycles.co.uk

FURTHER INFORMATION
- To view or print National Cycle Network routes, visit www.sustrans.org.uk
- Maps for this area are available to buy from www.sustransshop.co.uk
- Cambridge Tourist Information: 0871 226 8006; www.visitcambridge.org

ROUTE DESCRIPTION
At Jesus Green, head away from the city centre and under the dual carriageway along Riverside, beside the River Cam, passing through the city on the south side of the river. Continue along the traffic-free path through to Newmarket Road Park-and-Ride, before joining a roadside path that takes you alongside the Newmarket Road, under the A14 and out to the villages of Stow-cum-Quy and Bottisham. Turn left when you reach the high street at Bottisham and follow the Lode Road for 1.5 miles (2.5km) to Anglesey Abbey.

NEARBY CYCLE ROUTES
Cambridge has the highest proportion of cyclists in relation to its population in the UK, and there are a number of signed routes around the city, the most attractive ones being those that follow green corridors. Routes are of varying standards, and cyclists will need to look

Punting past Clare College on the River Cam

Anglesey Abbey

out for motorized traffic, pedestrians and other cyclists!

National Route 51 crosses Route 11 in Cambridge, then follows the Busway (Guided Bus) along a disused railway to St Ives. The previous Route 51 through the villages of Girton, Oakington and Longstanton remains an option, but the instigation of the Busway has allowed a largely traffic-free route to be opened. To the east of Cambridge, Route 11 runs along the opposite bank of the River Cam to the one that's followed in Route 51, but currently only as far as Waterbeach (see page 78).

GREAT SHELFORD TO WATERBEACH VIA CAMBRIDGE

The section between Great Shelford and Addenbrooke's Hospital marks the 10,000th mile of the National Cycle Network, opened in September 2005 by Sir John Sulston, the Nobel Prize-winning British scientist behind the Human Genome Project (see pages 4-5). The artwork along this route celebrates the role of the nearby Sanger Institute in decoding the vital human gene *BRCA2*. A series of stripes in four colours, representing the 10,257 genetic letters, or bases, of *BRCA2*, has been laid on the cyclepath using thermoplastic strips, heat-welded onto the tarmac. It is the sequence of the four bases, colour-coded – adenine (A) in green; cytosine (C) in blue; guanine (G) in yellow; and thymine (T) in red – that contains the code for life.

Four species of trees have also been planted at intervals along the route, to improve the local environment and to represent the colours of the four genome bases: yew (*Taxus baccata*), green; rowan (*Sorbus aucuparia* 'Sheerwater Seedling'), blue; crab apple (*Malus* 'Rudolph'), yellow; and cherry (*Prunus cerasifera* 'Nigra'), red.

The route continues from Addenbrooke's Hospital into Cambridge, with its stunning university colleges, and then follows the River Cam to Waterbeach, ending at the train station car park.

ROUTE INFORMATION

National Route: 11
Start: Shelford train station, Great Shelford.
Finish: Waterbeach train station.
Distance: 12 miles (19.5km). Shorter option, from Great Shelford to Cambridge 5 miles (8km).

Grade: Easy.
Surface: Tarmac or fine crushed stone on the towpath.
Hills: None.

King's College
Cambridge

Double Helix by Katy Hallett, Great Shelford

Trinity College quad, Cambridge

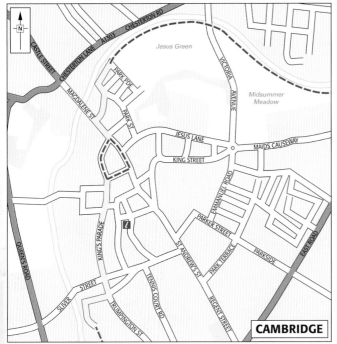

CAMBRIDGE

REFRESHMENTS
• Lots of choice in Cambridge.

THINGS TO SEE & DO
• University colleges; www.cam.ac.uk
• Fitzwilliam Museum: the collection includes paintings from the 14th century, sculpture, oriental art and antiquities from Egypt, the Ancient Near East, Greece, Rome and Cyprus; www.fitzmuseum.cam.ac.uk
• Cambridge Museum of Technology: based in the original sewage pumping station for Cambridge, the exhibits include the pumping station's original equipment and other engines; 01223 368650; www.museumoftechnology.com
• Nine Wells Nature reserve: between Shelford and Cambridge.

YOUNG & INEXPERIENCED CYCLISTS
The route is mainly traffic-free, but particular care is needed in Cambridge city centre, which is often very busy with pedestrians, cyclists, buses and taxis.

GREAT SHELFORD TO WATERBEACH VIA CAMBRIDGE

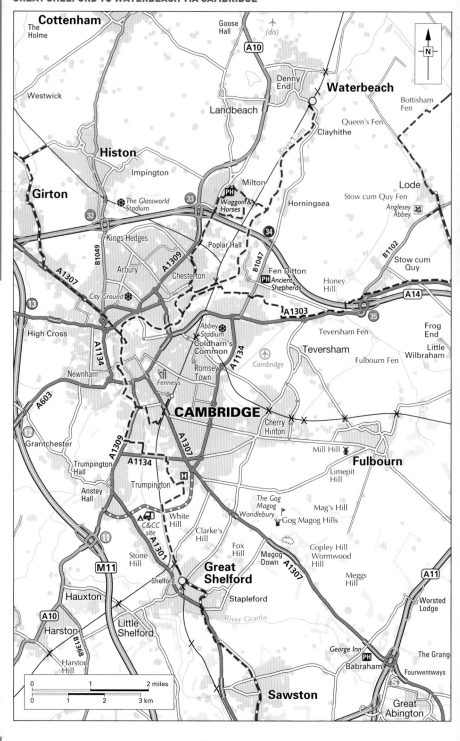

TRAIN STATIONS

Shelford; Cambridge; Waterbeach.

BIKE HIRE

- **City Cycle Hire, Cambridge:** 01223 365629; www.citycyclehire.com
- **Cambridge Station Cycles:** 01223 307125; www.stationcycles.co.uk

FURTHER INFORMATION

- To view or print National Cycle Network routes, visit www.sustrans.org.uk
- Maps for this area are available to buy from www.sustransshop.co.uk
- **Cambridge Tourist Information:** 0871 226 8006; www.visitcambridge.org

Emblem of Peterhouse College

ROUTE DESCRIPTION

Starting at Shelford train station, head northeast along Station Road, turning left into Chaston Road, which forms part of National Route 11. At the village edge, the route joins a path that follows the railway, with distinctive coloured stripes marking the 10,000th mile of the National Cycle Network.

At Addenbrooke's Hospital, the route joins roads and cyclepaths heading to Cambridge city centre, entering from the south at Granta Place. In the summer, this area is busy with students, tourists and locals, gathered around the many punts that moor here. The route then goes along King's Parade, past King's College, through the heart of the city, where there is plenty to see and do.

From Cambridge city centre, the route follows the River Cam to Waterbeach, crossing the river at the new Riverside bridge then following the towpath to Waterbeach, where a path leads to the station car park.

NEARBY CYCLE ROUTES

Cambridge has the highest number of cyclists per head of population in the UK, and you will soon realize that you are not alone. There are a number of signed routes around the city, with

the most attractive ones being those that follow green corridors. Routes are of varying standards, and cyclists will need to look out for motorized traffic, pedestrians and other cyclists! National Route 51 crosses route 11 in Cambridge, then follows the Cambridgeshire Guided Bus (Busway) along a disused railway to St Ives. The previous route through the villages of Girton, Oakington and Longstanton remains an option, but the opening of the guided Busway has enabled a largely traffic-free route. To the east of Cambridge, Route 51 runs along the opposite bank of the River Cam that's followed in Route 11 (see page 74), before heading east towards Newmarket.

'Genome Stripes' by Katy Hallett

BURY ST EDMUNDS TO THURSTON & STOWMARKET

Bury St Edmunds is an ancient town. St Edmund, for whom it was named, was King of the Angles, and killed when the Danes invaded in 869. Leave plenty of time to explore this fascinating place, and include a visit to East Anglia's oldest house (now a museum) and a drink in the Nutshell, which claims to be Britain's smallest pub.

From St Edmundsbury Cathedral, National Route 51 is traffic-free most of the way to the attractive village of Thurston. You can turn around or catch the train back from here, but you may well be tempted to continue along Route 51 as it winds along quiet Suffolk lanes to Stowmarket.

The route passes through the village of Woolpit, where the village sign shows a green boy and girl. The reason for this harks back to a local 12th-century legend when two mysterious green children appeared in the village, speaking no recognizable language. Part of the Swan Inn in the village is thought to date back to the 14th century. The village of Harleston is well worth exploring, its thatched church (just off the route) is beautiful both inside and out. Further on, Northfield Wood, just outside the village of Onehouse, is being lovingly replanted with broadleaf trees by the Woodland Trust and boasts a herd of deer.

Your ride ends at the bustling market town of Stowmarket, where you can explore the Museum of East Anglian Life. National Route 51 continues through Stowmarket to Needham Market and beyond.

ROUTE INFORMATION
National Route: 51
Start: St Edmundsbury Cathedral, Bury St Edmunds.
Finish: Stowmarket train station.
Distance: 17 miles (27.5km). Shorter option,
from St Edmundsbury Cathedral to Thurston
5 miles (8km).
Grade: Easy.
Surface: Tarmac paths and minor roads.
Hills: Fairly flat, with one steep climb at the start.

BURY ST EDMUNDS

THURSTON

Abbey ruins, Bury St Edmunds

YOUNG & INEXPERIENCED CYCLISTS

Mostly traffic-free from St Edmundsbury Cathedral to Thurston, then minor roads to Stowmarket.

REFRESHMENTS

- Lots of choice in Bury St Edmunds.
- Fox and Hounds pub, Thurston.
- The Orchard Room, cafe/restaurant, Thurston.
- The Bull pub, Woolpit.
- Lots of choice in Stowmarket.

Great Gate, Bury St Edmunds Abbey

THINGS TO SEE & DO

- **St Edmundsbury Cathedral:** for over 1,000 years a site of worship; vaulted ceilings and medieval altarpiece; 01284 748720; www.stedscathedral.co.uk/
- **Moyse's Hall Museum:** local history in a Norman town house; 01284 757160; www.stedmundsbury.gov.uk/moyseshall
- **St Edmunds Abbey:** wealthiest and most powerful Benedictine monastery in England; complete 14th-century Great Gate and Norman Tower; www.stedmundsbury.gov.uk
- **Museum of East Anglian Life, Stowmarket:** beautiful 75-acre site. East Anglian crafts and traditional gypsy culture; 15 splendidly restored historic buildings; bistro serving local produce; 01449 612229; www.eastanglianlife.org.uk

STOWMARKET

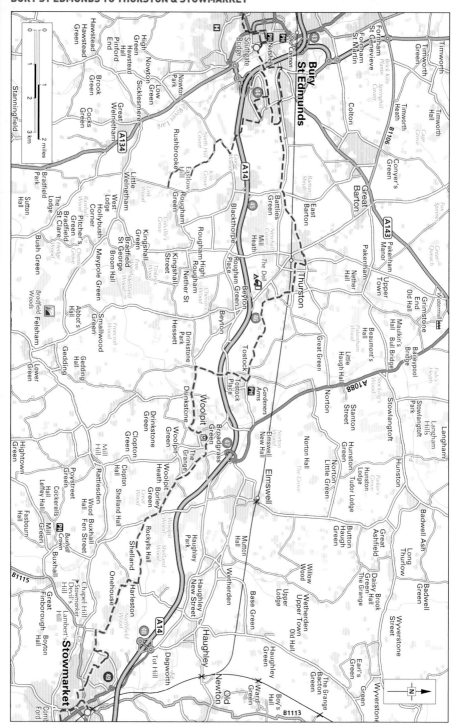

Village sign depicting local legend

Norman Tower, Bury St Edmunds

TRAIN STATIONS
Bury St Edmunds; Thurston; Stowmarket.

BIKE HIRE
None locally.

FURTHER INFORMATION
- To view or print National Cycle Network routes, visit www.sustrans.org.uk
- Maps for this area are available to buy from www.sustransshop.co.uk
- Bury St Edmunds Tourist Information: 01284 764667; www.visit-burystedmunds.co.uk

ROUTE DESCRIPTION
The route from Bury St Edmunds station to the cathedral is not yet signed. Turn left out of the station and right onto Fornham Road, cross the main road at the pedestrian crossing and go left down Cotton Lane to the T-junction at the end. Turn right, go round Abbey Gate and down Angel Hill, to turn left at the Norman Tower by the Cathedral onto National Route 51.

From the Cathedral itself, the route is well signposted as you head east out of town, over the A14. Take care as you cross at East Barton Road, just before the village of Thurston. You may choose to stop at Thurston, if only for refreshments. To carry on, make your way east through the village on to Church Road and go under the railway track. Stay on-road until you are signposted to Woolpit, where there's another chance to stop. From here, it's on-road all the way to Stowmarket. To find the station turn left and ride or wheel your bike along the B1115. There are direct trains between Bury St Edmunds and Stowmarket.

NEARBY CYCLE ROUTES
National Route 51 carries on through Ipswich and beyond to Felixstowe.

In a westerly direction, National Route 51 follows minor roads between Bury St Edmunds and Newmarket, although the first section from Bury St Edmunds uses some busier roads. The route continues from Newmarket to Cambridge.

THETFORD TO WATTON

Thetford has history oozing from its walls. An ancient market town, it is filled with heritage sites, quiet gardens, open parkland and a relaxing riverside. With Thetford Forest right on the doorstep, it is also the best base for discovering the wildlife and outdoor pleasures of The Brecks.

In its heyday, Thetford could boast being the Saxon capital of East Anglia – in the 10th century it was a town worthy of its own mint, and its coins have been found as far afield as Scandinavia.

This route takes you along Peddars Way, through The Brecks, a unique landscape of heath, pine forests and large open fields. You could walk some of the Great Eastern Pingo Trail in Hockham Heath and use the forest tracks to pick up Peddars Way at almost any point – it is all well signposted. There are even a couple of picnic sites. The areas inside the Nature Reserves and the full length of the disused railway line are a delight.

Watton – a bustling market town with 18 historic and beautiful churches, and ancient Wayland Wood, noted for its bluebells – lies at the heart of the Breckland area. It is said to be where two small babes were abandoned in the 16th century, the provenance of the folk tale *Babes in the Wood*. There are claims that their ghosts can still be seen in the woods today. This is commemorated in the town sign in front of the hand-wound clock tower in Watton High Street.

A forest clearing, at Thetford Warren

ROUTE INFORMATION

National Route: 13
Start: Thetford train station.
Finish: Watton High Street.
Distance: 15 miles (24km).

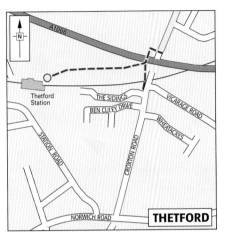

Grade: Mostly easy; moderate on dirt section.
Surface: Tarmac paths and minor roads. Some unsurfaced roads for 2 miles (3km), which are potholed in places.
Hills: Mainly flat, but a mild descent at Croxton.

YOUNG & INEXPERIENCED CYCLISTS

Easy-going, mainly quiet minor roads, but care should still be taken.

REFRESHMENTS

- A number of options in Thetford.
- Dog & Partridge, Wretham.
- Chequers Inn, Thompson.
- A number of options in Watton town centre.

THINGS TO SEE & DO

- Five self-guide town trails to choose from: *Heritage, Thomas Paine, Dad's Army, Maharajah Duleep Singh* and *Haunted Trail*; www.explorethetford.co.uk/trails.aspx
- **Ancient House Museum:** story of Thetford and The Brecks; 01842 752599; www.museums.norfolk.gov.uk
- **Thetford Priory:** remains of one of the most important East Anglian monasteries; www.english-heritage.org.uk
- **High Lodge Forest Centre:** walk, cycle, play, picnic, barbecue or simply relax and enjoy

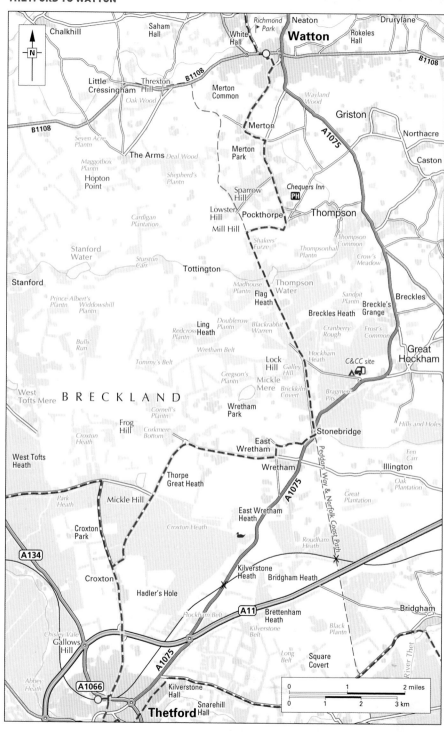

Wayland Wood is noted for its bluebells

the forest; 01842 815434;
www.forestry.gov.uk/highlodge

TRAIN STATIONS
Thetford.

BIKE HIRE
• High Lodge Forest Centre: 01842 810090;
  www.forestry.gov.uk/highlodge

FURTHER INFORMATION
• To view or print National Cycle Network
  routes, visit www.sustrans.org.uk
• Maps for this area are available to buy from
  www.sustransshop.co.uk
• Thetford Tourist Information: 01842 751975;
  www.explorethetford.co.uk
• BrecksTourist Information: 01362 656870;
  www.brecks.org.uk

ROUTE DESCRIPTION
Come out of Thetford station on the Norwich-
bound side, and take the path leading directly to
the route from the platform. It's a longer way
round on road from the main station entrance
but you soon meet Route 13 on Croxton Road.
Follow this road for a while, under the A11.

Go through the village of Croxton. Ignoring
the sign for Regional Route 30, turn right into
Croxton Heath. Make your way safely through
the Thorpe Camp military range towards
Wretham. Just as you get to the village, turn
left onto Church Road and stay on that road,
veering right as you go. Turn left onto the
shared pavement by the A1075, past the Dog
& Partridge pub, then turn left off the A1075
down a quiet tarred road that becomes
untarred through the forest. Follow the signs.
This section can be potholed (and muddy after
rain) due to farm and army vehicles. The
viewpoint to your right at Thompson Water
allows you to see a display of all sorts of
birdlife. Continue on the posted route, then
rejoin a tarred road towards Thompson. Once
through Thompson, the route to Watton, which
takes you through the attractive village of
Merton, is signposted all the way.

NEARBY CYCLE ROUTES
National Route 13 continues north to join Route
1 just south of Fakenham in Norfolk.

Thetford Forest is a large forest a few miles
northwest of Thetford. Run by the Forestry
Commission, it has many tracks running
through it, making it a brilliant place to cycle
off-road. The forest contains four cycling
routes: the green family route, the blue route
and the more challenging red and black routes.

ELY TO WICKEN FEN

Charming and historic Ely, the third smallest city in England, is the starting point of this route. The cathedral that gives it city status is known as the Ship of the Fens and has its origins in a convent and monastery founded by Ethedreda in 673. The cathedral building itself dates from the 12th century. Ely was home to the Lord Protector, Oliver Cromwell, for a decade in the 17th century. He is reputed to have closed the cathedral and stabled his horses there. Another earlier famous anti-monarchist son was the Anglo-Saxon leader Hereward the Wake, who was said to have roamed the fens organizing resistance to William the Conqueror.

Upon leaving Ely, the ride is characterized by big skies and an uncluttered landscape as you make your way towards Wicken Fen National Nature Reserve. This is the National Trust's oldest nature reserve, and England's most famous fen. It is home to wild ponies, otters and rare butterflies and birds, and has wildlife trails and hides.

At the visitor centre, you will find information about many National Trust projects, including The Wicken Fen Vision, which is their most ambitious habitat restoration project. The plan is to create a new nature reserve covering around 22 square miles (57 sq.km) between Cambridge and Wicken Fen. It is thought it will take up to 100 years to complete.

ROUTE INFORMATION

National Route: 11
Start: Ely Cathedral.
Finish: Visitor Centre, Wicken Fen National Nature Reserve.

Distance: 8 miles (13km).
Grade: Easy.
Surface: Tarmac, with a short section of stone farm track.
Hills: None.

Windmill at Wicken Fen

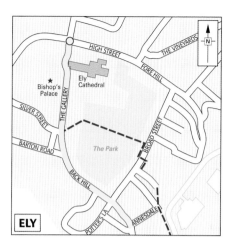

Ely Cathedral

YOUNG & INEXPERIENCED CYCLISTS

The route southwards out of Ely is mostly traffic-free, with some short on-road sections. Care is needed crossing the A142.

REFRESHMENTS

- Lots of choice in Ely.
- Maid's Head pub, Wicken.
- Cafe at Wicken Fen National Nature Reserve.

THINGS TO SEE & DO

- **Ely Cathedral:** founded in the 12th century; 01353 667735; www.elycathedral.org
- **Stained Glass Museum:** located in the cathedral; unique collection of stained glass, dating back to medieval times; library, shop and events programme; 01353 660347; www.stainedglassmuseum.com
- **Ely Museum:** located in the Bishop's Gaol,

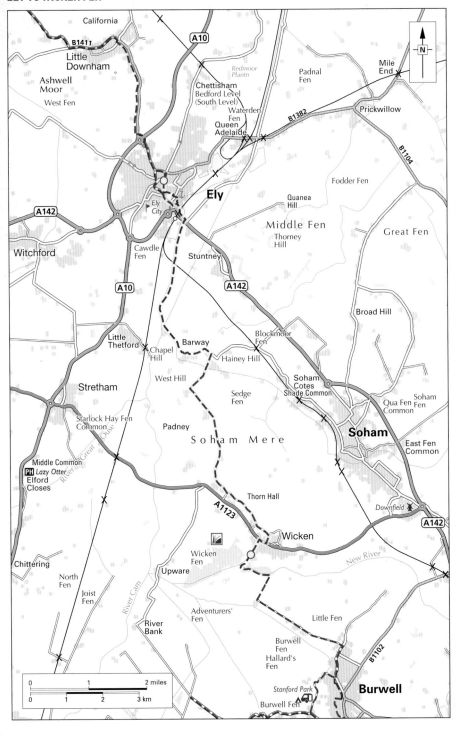

California
B1411
Little
Downham
Ashwell
Moor
West Fen
A10
Redmoor
Plantn
Chettisham
Bedford Level
(South Level)
Waterden
Fen
Queen
Adelaide
Padnal
Fen
B1382
Prickwillow
Mile
End
B1104
Fodder Fen
Ely
Ely
City
A142
Witchford
Cawdle
Fen
Stuntney
Quanea
Hill
Middle Fen
Thorney
Hill
Great Fen
A10
A142
Broad Hill
Little
Thetford
Chapel
Hill
Barway
Blockmoor
Fen
Hainey Hill
Stretham
West Hill
Sedge
Fen
Soham
Cotes
Shade Common
Soham
Fen
Common
Qua Fen
Common
Soham
Starlock Hay Fen
Common
Padney
S o h a m   M e r e
East Fen
Common
Middle Common
PH *Lazy Otter*
Elford
Closes
Thorn Hall
A1123
Downfield
A142
Chittering
North
Fen
Joist
Fen
Wicken
Fen
Upware
Wicken
New River
A142
Adventurers'
Fen
Little Fen
River
Bank
Burwell
Fen
Hallard's
Fen
B1102
Stanford Park
Burwell Fen
Burwell

0   1   2 miles
0 1 2 3 km

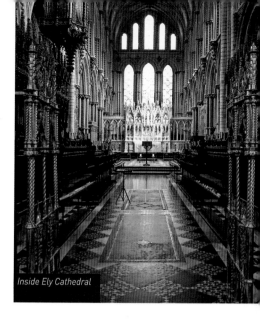

Inside Ely Cathedral

this is the history centre for the Isle of Ely and the Fens; displays include original prison cells, fossils that can be touched, Roman remains and an archive film of the Fens; 01353 666655; www.elymuseum.org.uk

- Oliver Cromwell's House, Ely: the only surviving former Cromwell residence other than Hampton Court; recreated to show how his family would have lived in the mid-17th century; 01353 662062; www.visitely.eastcambs.gov.uk

- Wicken Fen National Nature Reserve: internationally important wetland nature reserve; the wooden working windpump and traditional fen cottage provide an insight into the social history of the fens; 01353 720274; www.wicken.org.uk

- Burwell Museum of Fen Edge Village Life: includes a windmill, working forge, Victorian schoolroom, World War II display in a Nissen Hut and other exhibits about local life in the past; closed Nov-Easter 01638 605544; www.burwellmuseum-org-uk-.ik.com

TRAIN STATIONS
Ely.

BIKE HIRE
- Ely Cycles, Ely: 01353 668551; www.elycycles.co.uk

FURTHER INFORMATION
- To view or print National Cycle Network routes, visit www.sustrans.org.uk
- Maps for this area are available to buy from www.sustransshop.co.uk
- Cambridge Cycling Campaign: www.camcycle.org.uk
- Ely and East Cambridgeshire Tourist Information: 01353 662062; www.visitely.eastcambs.gov.uk

ROUTE DESCRIPTION
Starting at Ely Cathedral, turn left down the Gallery (the road running in front of the cathedral). This turns into Back Hill. Take the second turn on the left, Annesdale, towards the river, and just before the railway station. Watch out for ducks who have made this area their home. Turn right onto the riverside path and follow this under the railway. The route southwards out of Ely is mostly traffic-free, with some short on-road sections. After crossing the A142 (please take care) you are soon beside the River Great Ouse on a traffic-free route built by a Sustrans work camp in 2005. Go through the tiny village of Barway, past the famously ghostly Spinney Abbey on one side and Soham Mere on the other, towards Wicken. Turn right onto the high street, which can be busy, and then turn left, heading for Wicken Fen, a national nature reserve with a rich variety of plants, birds, mammals and insects.

NEARBY CYCLE ROUTES
National Route 11 carries on from Wicken along straight, quiet roads to the tidy village of Burwell. Here, it meets Route 51, just west of Burwell, where a left turn and a circuitous 7-mile (11-km) ride takes you to Newmarket. Taking a right turn will bring you to Cambridge 13 miles (21km) later. Both routes begin on minor roads and end with largely traffic-free entry to your chosen destination.

ST IVES TO HUNTINGDON & GRAFHAM WATER

St Ives, known as Slepe in Saxon times, is an ancient riverside market town in the old county of Huntingdonshire. It changed its name after the body of the Persian Bishop St Ivo was found buried in the town. It stands on the River Great Ouse and is famous for the 13th-century Chapel on the Bridge. The St Ives settlement was developed by the monks of Ramsey Abbey, who built the town's first bridge, a wooden structure, in 1107. In 1414, it was decided to replace it with a stone arch bridge. The chapel was added in 1426.

Houghton Mill is an 18th-century water mill set upon an island in the river in the village of Houghton, just north of the route. A National Trust property, it is well worth a look at, as is the fascinating town of Huntingdon, the birthplace of Oliver Cromwell. There are also some magnificent walks to be had down the Ouse Valley Way.

The nature reserve that surrounds Grafham Water reservoir contains ancient and plantation woodlands, grasslands and wetland habitats. It is one of the prime bird-watching sites in the county, with rare and scarce birds, such as osprey and the occasional Slavonian grebe, alongside the more familiar resident mallards and greylag geese. With 9 miles (14.5km) of shoreline and around 170 species of bird recorded each year, there is always something to see.

ROUTE INFORMATION
National Route: 51
Start: Bridge Street, St Ives.
Finish: Visitor Centre, Grafham Water.
Distance: 13 miles (21km).
Grade: Easy.

Surface: Tarmac roads and gravel tracks.
Hills: None.

YOUNG & INEXPERIENCED CYCLISTS
The route between Hemingford Abbots and Godmanchester is largely traffic-free, as is the route between Huntingdon and Brampton, although it follows a main road. Grafham Water is especially good for novice cyclists.

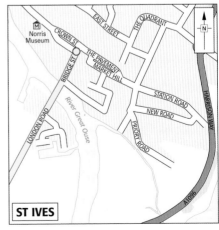

Bridge with its own chapel at St Ives

REFRESHMENTS

- Lots of choice in Huntingdon.
- Cafe and picnic areas at Hinchingbrooke Country Park.
- Cafe at The Grafham Water Visitor Centre.
- The Wheatsheaf, Perry, south of reservoir.

THINGS TO SEE & DO

- **Chapel of St Ledger, St Ives:** also known as the Chapel on the Bridge, located on the ancient stone bridge over the River Great Ouse; it can be viewed by obtaining a key from the Town Hall or the Norris Museum; 01480 497314; www.norrismuseum.org.uk
- **Cromwell Museum, Huntingdon:** the Lord Protector of England's former grammar school, now a museum recording his life; 01480 375830; www.cambridgeshire.gov.uk
- **Hinchingbrooke Country Park:** 170 acres of open grasslands, meadows, woodlands and lakes, with a wealth of wildlife everywhere; 01480 451568; www.huntsdc.gov.uk
- **Portholme Meadow:** west of Godmanchester, the largest ancient water meadow in the UK.
- **Grafham Water Nature Reserve:** expanse of open water, surrounded by wetlands, grasslands and ancient woods with a huge range of birds; 01954 713500; www.wildlifebcnp.org
- **Grafham Water Centre:** provides land- and water-based activities and courses; 0845 634 6022; www.grafham-water-centre.co.uk

TRAIN STATIONS

Huntingdon.

BIKE HIRE

- Rutland Cycling, Grafham Water, Marlow Car Park: 01480 812500; www.rutlandcycling.com

HUNTINGDON

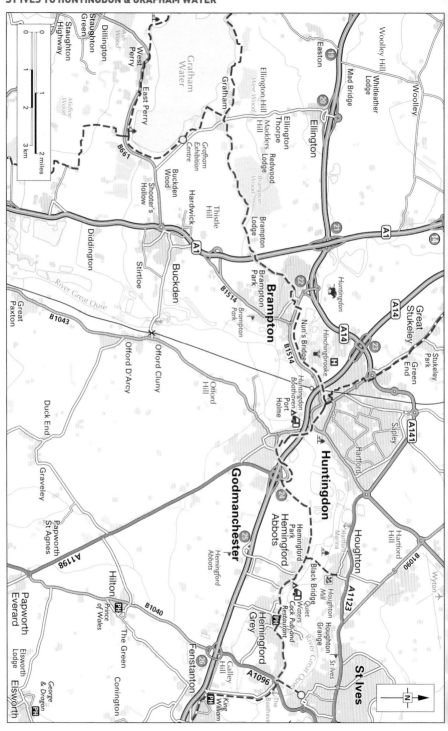

This route is good for watching wildlife

FURTHER INFORMATION

- To view or print National Cycle Network routes, visit www.sustrans.org.uk
- Maps for this area are available to buy from www.sustransshop.co.uk
- **Huntingdonshire Tourist Information:** 01480 388388; www.visithuntingdonshire.org

ROUTE DESCRIPTION

Starting at Bridge Street, cross the River Great Ouse on the 15th-century stone bridge, still in use but cars are restricted. Continue onto London Road. Take the first right down Hemingford Road, along National Route 51. Stay on the road until you get to Hemingford Grey. Continue on the signposted route until you get to Hemingford Abbots. The High Street becomes Common Lane, leading to Godmanchester Eastside Common, which includes an attractive traffic-free path across the Common to Cow Lane. Turn left past the sewage works and into Godmanchester. Follow the route through Godmanchester and Huntingdon partly on-road and partly off-road. Going through Huntingdon's pedestrianised town centre will involved walking in places. The route takes you past Huntingdon station and then to Brampton Road (B1514) and the start of a long, traffic-free section to Brampton. Use the shared cycleway and footpath, with the Country Park on the right, into Brampton, keeping on the path past the major roundabout into Church Road. At Grove Lane, cross the B1514 and head into the village, turning right into the High Street. Pass the village green and continue straight on, past fields, to cross the bridge over the A1. Entering Grafham village, turn right at the T-junction and immediately left into Church Hill. At the end of Church Hill, follow the cyclepath to the left to reach the visitor centre. If you wish to ride around Grafham Water, this is a circuit of 9 miles (14 km). It is advisable to go anticlockwise as this avoids a right turn on the B661.

NEARBY CYCLE ROUTES

National Route 12 carries on north from Huntingdon to Peterborough and Spalding, and south to St Neots.

The Busway links Huntingdon, St Ives and Cambridge, and forms the longest guided bus route in the world. From St Ives to Cambridge, there is a bridle path that forms part of National Route 51.

MARCH TO WISBECH

March was once an island surrounded by marshes. Now it is a busy market town on the course of the old River Nene, which winds its way through the centre, past the park and pretty riverside gardens. The river is often busy, with colourful narrowboats cruising the Fenland Waterways. March has its own saint, Wendreda, and the church bearing her name has a beautiful late 15th-century double hammerbeam roof, said to be the finest of its kind, with over 120 angels. John Betjeman described the church as 'worth cycling 40 miles in a headwind to see'.

The Hereward Way long-distance trail and the Woodman's Way, a 6.5-mile/10.5-km circular walk around March and Wimblington, make this a wonderful area for walking and cycling. The Fens Cycle Way gives an opportunity to visit this unique landscape, with its numerous nature reserves, windmills, museums, churches and historic market towns – not to mention the glorious countryside with panoramic views and stunning sunsets.

Wisbech, at the end of the route, claims to be the capital of the Fens and has some of the finest Georgian streets in Britain. It had served as a port since medieval times, but when the estuary of the River Ouse silted up in the 17th century it was diverted into the sea at Lynn, and the present artificial course of the River Nene was constructed from Peterborough to The Wash. .

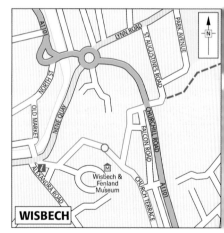

ROUTE INFORMATION
National Route: 63
Start: March train station.
Finish: Wisbech Market Square.
Distance: 11 miles (17.5km).
Grade: Easy.
Surface: Tarmac roads and fine stone paths.
Hills: None. However, it's worth checking the wind direction. With no hills, cycling in the Fens with a strong headwind can be arduous.

YOUNG & INEXPERIENCED CYCLISTS
This route uses a combination of roads and paths. The first section of road along Hundred Road can have some heavy traffic, but after that the roads are generally quiet until the end, apart from a short section around Ring's End and again along Main Road.

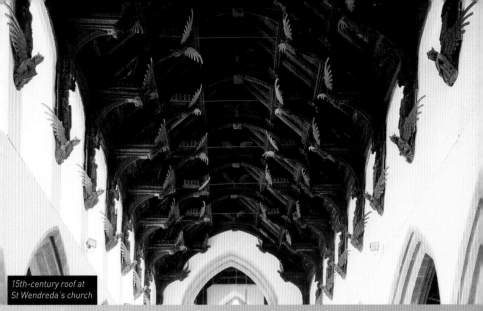

15th-century roof at St Wendreda's church

Riverside houses at Wisbech

REFRESHMENTS

- Lots of choice in March and Wisbech.
- The Sportsman pub, Elm.
- Licensed tea-room at Peckover House, Wisbech.

THINGS TO SEE & DO

- **March Museum:** displays showing Fenland life over the past 100 years, housed in an old school; 01354 655300; www.marchmuseum.co.uk
- **Peckover House, Wisbech:** elegant Georgian merchant's house by the river, with beautiful walled garden; 01945 583463; www.nationaltrust.org.uk
- **Wisbech & Fenland Museum:** home to two historic libraries and a substantial archive, concerning the natural and cultural heritage

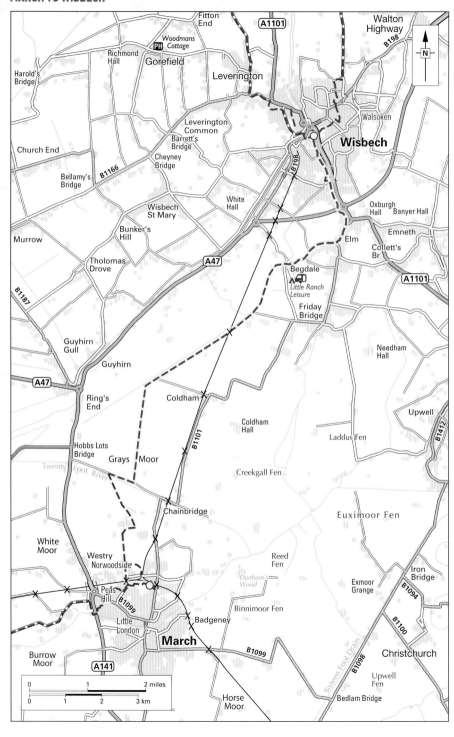

of Wisbech and the surrounding Fenland;
01945 583817; www.wisbechmuseum.org.uk
- **Elgoods Brewery, Wisbech:** real ale brewery;
  visitors can follow the traditional brewing
  process and sample a variety of ales;
  01945 583160; www.elgoods-brewery.co.uk

TRAIN STATIONS
March.

BIKE HIRE
None locally.

FURTHER INFORMATION
- To view or print National Cycle Network
  routes, visit www.sustrans.org.uk
- Maps for this area are available to buy from
  www.sustransshop.co.uk
- **The Fens Tourist Information:** Wisbech
  tourist info centre; 01945 583263
  www.fenland.gov.uk

ROUTE DESCRIPTION
Turn right out of March train station through
the car park and towards the signposted
National Route 63. The route passes a small
recreation ground before joining Robin
Goodfellow's Lane. Turn right at the T-junction
and proceed down Norwood Road, over a level
crossing. Continue straight along Hundred
Road, which gradually gets quieter until you see
Whitemoor Prison. Turn right onto Longhill
Road and go left after the prison building.
Continue on a stretch of traffic-free path until
you hit the busy road into Ring's End. Turn right
onto Twenty Foot Road, taking care as you do
so. Take the first left onto the less busy
Graysmoor Drove. Then turn right onto Long
Drove and make your way towards Begdale. Go
straight over the crossroads down Belt Drove
and continue down the Begdale Road until you
reach the village of Elm. Turn left at Elm
Church and go along the potentially busy Main
Road for a short spell. Turn off onto Low Road
and follow this into Wisbech. Negotiate the

*Angels on St
Wendreda's church*

one-way system at Weasenham Lane to take
you back onto the Elm Road. Follow the
signposted route to Wisbech Market Square.

NEARBY CYCLE ROUTES
A mixture of quiet roads and well-surfaced
tracks, the Fens Cycle Way consists of two
separate loops. The Northern route, 40 miles
(64.5km) long, starts in Wisbech; the Southern
route, 34 miles (55.5km) long, in Ely. The two
are connected by a 9-mile (14.5-km) link. The
full route is designed to take between two and
four days, making it suitable for both the
experienced and leisure cyclist. It also connects
with National Route 1 (Hull to Harwich) and
National Route 63 (Wisbech to Peterborough).

PETERBOROUGH GREEN WHEEL

The concept of Peterborough's Green Wheel is a 45-mile (72.5-km) network of routes in and around the city, including a 'rim', a 'hub' and 'spokes'. The ride described here initially runs west from the city centre, following the River Nene to Ferry Meadows Country Park, the entrance to which is marked by a wonderful centurion/frog/kingfisher/swan statue.

You'll also visit the pretty villages of Marholm and Etton. Marholm's village sign represents all sectors of Marholm's community under the Fitzwilliam family coat of arms and motto – *Appetitus Rationi Pareat* ('May your desires be reasoned').

Before you set off, or on your return, make the effort to visit Peterborough's splendid cathedral, one of England's finest Norman buildings, begun in 1118, and with a magnificent west front.

Peterborough Cathedral

ROUTE INFORMATION

National Route: 12, 63; Regional Route 21
Start and Finish: The south end of Bridge Street in the centre of Peterborough; the junction of Routes 12, 53 and 63. The route can also be easily accessed from Peterborough train station, by heading north beside the railway and following signs leading to Route 12.
Distance: 21-mile (34-km) circular route.
Grade: Easy.
Surface: Tarmac or fine gravel paths.
Hills: None.

Bluebells in Ferry Meadows Country Park

YOUNG & INEXPERIENCED CYCLISTS

The best section for novices and young children is from the riverside path in the centre of Peterborough to the stone bridge over the River Nene at the western end of Ferry Meadows Country Park. This is traffic-free and flat.

REFRESHMENTS

- Lots of choice in Peterborough.
- The Boathouse pub, near the rowing lake.
- Two cafes at Ferry Meadows Country Park.
- Fitzwilliam Arms pub, Marholm.
- Golden Pheasant pub, Etton.
- Bluebell pub, Glinton.

THINGS TO SEE & DO

- **Peterborough Cathedral:** 01733 343342; www.peterborough-cathedral.org.uk

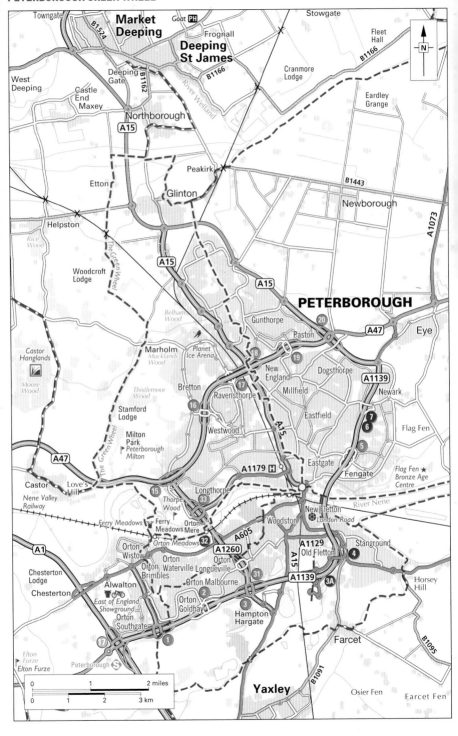

Towngate

Market Deeping

Goat PH

Stowgate

B1524

Frognall

Fleet Hall

Deeping St James

B1166

Cranmore Lodge

B1166

Eardley Grange

West Deeping

Deeping Gate

B1162

A1073

Castle End Maxey

Northborough

A15

River Welland

Peakirk

B1443

Etton

Glinton

Newborough

Helpston

A15

Rice Wood

The Green Wheel

A15

PETERBOROUGH

Woodcroft Lodge

Gunthorpe

20

A47

Eye

Paston

Castor Hanglands

Belham Wood

Marholm

Planet Ice Arena

18

19

Dogsthorpe

A1139

Moore Wood

Mucklands Wood

Bretton

New England

Newark

Thistlemoor Wood

17

Ravensthorpe

Millfield

Eastfield

Flag Fen

Stamford Lodge

16

Westwood

7

6

Milton Park

Peterborough Milton

A15

Eastgate

5

A47

A1179

H

Fengate

Flag Fen ★ Bronze Age Centre

Castor

Love's Hill

15

Thorpe Wood

Longthorpe

River Nene

Nene Valley Railway

33

Woodston

New Fletton

Ferry Meadows

Ferry Meadows Mere

Orton Meadows

London Road

A1

Orton Wistow

32

A605

A1129

Stanground

Chesterton Lodge

Orton Brimbles

Orton Waterville

Orton Longueville

A1260

Old Fletton

4

Chesterton

Alwalton

East of England Showground

Orton Malbourne

31

A15

3A

Horsey Hill

Orton Goldhay

2

A1139

Orton Southgate

1

3

Hampton Hargate

Farcet

B1095

17

Peterborough S

Elton Furze

Elton Furze

Farcet Fen

Yaxley

B1091

Osier Fen

0 ——— 1 ——— 2 miles
0 —— 1 —— 2 —— 3 km

The River Nene at Peterborough

- **Peterborough Sculpture Park:** includes an early Antony Gormley piece; www.peterboroughsculpture.org
- **Longthorpe Tower:** just off the route, to the west of Peterborough; www.english-heritage.org.uk
- **Ferry Meadows Country Park:** lakes, meadows and woodlands; 01733 234193; www.nene-park-trust.org.uk
- **Nene Valley Railway:** steam train rides from Peterborough Nene Valley station to Wansford station, a return trip of 15 miles (24km); 01780 784444; www.nvr.org.uk
- **Flag Fen Bronze Age Centre:** just off the route, near Shanks Millennium Bridge; 0844 4140646; www.english-heritage.org.uk

TRAIN STATIONS
Peterborough.

BIKE HIRE
- **Lakeside Leisure:** 01733 234418; www.lakesideleisure.com

FURTHER INFORMATION
- To view or print National Cycle Network routes, visit www.sustrans.org.uk
- Maps for this area are available to buy from www.sustransshop.co.uk

- **Peterborough Tourist Information:** 01733 452336; www.visitpeterborough.com

ROUTE DESCRIPTION
This ride runs west from the city centre on the 'spoke' signed as Route 63, following the River Nene, past the rowing lake and the Nene Valley Railway Line to Ferry Meadows Country Park.

After following traffic-free trails up to this point, you join the network of quiet lanes linking the pretty villages of Marholm and Etton. The second part of the ride follows the 'rim' of the Green Wheel as far as Glinton, then uses another 'spoke', Route 12, through Werrington, which is largely on urban cycle lanes, to return to the pedestrianized heart of the city.

OTHER NEARBY CYCLE ROUTES
Peterborough is at a crossroads of the National Cycle Network: Route 63 goes from Wisbech to Leicester; Route 12 from London to Spalding; and Route 53 from Kettering into the centre of Peterborough. The distinct blue and white signs of Regional Route 21 designate the Peterborough Green Wheel, which overlaps with all three National Cycle Network routes.

BECCLES TO LOWESTOFT NESS

This route begins in the charming town of Beccles, and takes you through the Suffolk countryside to Lowestoft Ness, which is the most easterly point in the British Isles.

Beccles, situated on the River Waveney, was once a flourishing Saxon seaport and is still a popular boating place today. It has a 14th-century church with an imposing detached 16th-century bell tower, which serves as a landmark for miles around.

Lowestoft, once a busy fishing port, is now among the leading areas in the UK for renewable energy. It started in 2005 with the installation of the UK's largest wind turbine, at 80m (262ft) tall, which generates energy for the national grid. Over the next ten years, more than £10 billion will be invested in the east of England coastline for offshore renewable energy. The award-winning OrbisEnergy Centre was completed in 2009, and there are plans for the world's largest offshore wind farm 15 miles (24km) from the Suffolk coast.

As well as its fishing history, Lowestoft is also famous for its porcelain. Previously made in the 18th century, it was recently put back into production, with a new factory, shop and information centre on Battery Green Road. The Lowestoft Porcelain Trail is also a must for discovering the story of china production in the town, with ancient buildings depicting the story through time. Displays of many original pieces can be found at Lowestoft Museum in Broad House, Oulton Broad.

ROUTE INFORMATION
National Route: 1
Regional Route: 30
Start: Beccles train station.
Finish: Lowestoft Ness.
Distance: 14 miles (22.5km)
Grade: Easy.
Surface: Tarmac.

Hills: Minor hills along the way, but mainly flat.

YOUNG & INEXPERIENCED CYCLISTS
Both ends of the route go through towns and a

The River Waveney at Beccles

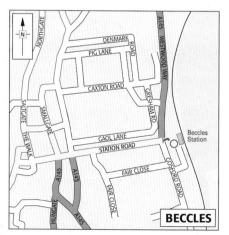

BECCLES

lot of the journey is on road, albeit fairly small country roads.

REFRESHMENTS
- Lots of choice in Beccles.
- The Three Horseshoes pub, North Cove.
- Lots of choice in Lowestoft.

THINGS TO SEE & DO
- **Beccles Museum:** specializes in local history, local trades and Victoriana, housed in a 16th-century Grade 1 listed building; 01502 715722; www.becclesmuseum.org.uk
- **East Anglia Transport Museum, Carlton Colville:** working museum where visitors can ride on trams, trolley-buses and narrow-gauge trains among others; 01502 518459; www.eatm.org.uk
- **Carlton Marshes:** 100 acres of grazing marsh, fens and peat pools; 01502 564250
- **Oulton Broad:** fine stretch of inland water, perfect for sailing, rowing or walking.
- **Lowestoft Museum:** the most extensive collection of Lowestoft Porcelain; summer opening only; www.lowestoftmuseum.org

- **Lowestoft beaches:** both North and South Beaches have Blue Flag status.

TRAIN STATIONS
Beccles; Lowestoft.

BIKE HIRE
- **Outney Meadow Caravan Park:** 01986 892338; www.outneymeadow.co.uk

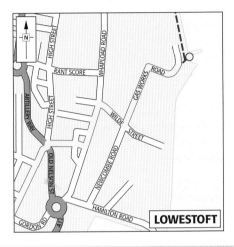

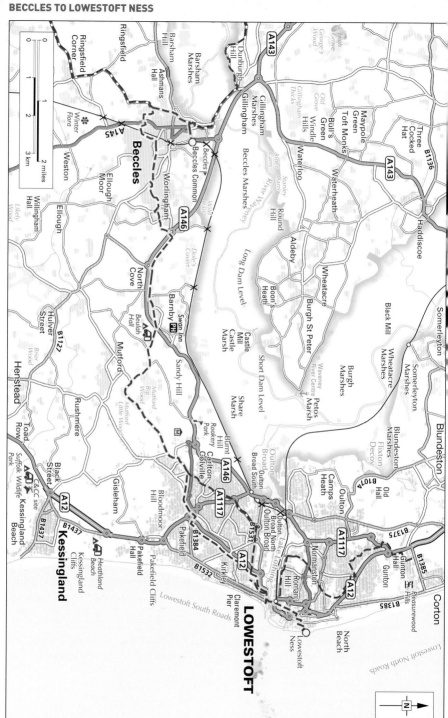

Winter solstice plaque, Lowestoft

- Martha's Cottage Cycle Hire: 01502 476789;
  www.marthascottagecyclehire.co.uk
- Michael's Cycles, Beccles: 01502 717413

FURTHER INFORMATION

- To view or print National Cycle Network
  routes, visit www.sustrans.org.uk
- Maps for this area are available to buy from
  www.sustransshop.co.uk
- Beccles Tourist Information: 01502 713196;
  www.beccles.info
- Lowestoft Tourist Information: 01502 533600;
  www.visit-lowestoft.co.uk

ROUTE DESCRIPTION

From Beccles station, cross straight over
Gosford Road and go along Station Road to the
town centre, where you will have to follow the
one-way system until you reach National Route
1. Head south past St Michaels Church along
Ballygate and Ringsfield Road, before turning
left after Sir John Leman High School. Here,
Regional Route 30 leaves National Route 1.
Route 30 follows residential roads and paths
through Worlingham towards the point where
the Lowestoft Road meets the A146. Cross
straight over the roundabout to join a quiet road
parallel to the A146. It's on-road from here until
you reach The Three Horseshoe pub on the

approach to North Cove. You may want to take
advantage of this 15th-century coaching house
for refreshments. A traffic-free track takes you
into North Cove and then it's back on-road all
the way to Lowestoft. Be careful when you leave
Barnby to cross the A146.

As you get into the town, the route becomes
National Route 1 at Carlton Colville and is
clearly signposted to Lowestoft station. To
reach Lowestoft Ness from there, follow the
signed North Sea Cycle Route.

NEARBY CYCLE ROUTES

Regional Route 30 (The Two Rivers Cycle Route)
of the National Cycle Network runs north from
Lowestoft to King's Lynn and west from
Beccles to Diss and Thetford.

Regional Route 31 is signed from Gillingham
(near Beccles), where it leaves National Route 1
to Reedham Ferry in Norfolk. Route 1 goes
north from Beccles to Norwich (see page 110)
and beyond. To the south, it goes to Colchester.

You can start the North Sea Cycle Route
from Beccles. At 3,730 miles (6,000km), it's
the world's longest cycle route:
www.northsea-cycle.com

BECCLES TO WHITLINGHAM COUNTRY PARK

This 24-mile (38.5-km) section of National Route 1 takes you through the Norfolk Broads and close to, or along, the Wherryman's Way. It starts in Suffolk in the charming town of Beccles, perched on the River Waveney, passing through Loddon and Chedgrave as it hugs the River Yare towards the city of Norwich. The Wherryman's Way is a 35-mile (56.5-km) recreational route, which takes its name from the wherry, a large cargo-carrying barge which was once a common sight on these waters.

Norwich has a wealth of historical architecture and claims with some justification to be the most complete medieval city in Britain. It is dominated by its magnificent Norman cathedral, boasting the largest cloisters in England, the second tallest spire in the country and an amazing 1,200 carved stone roof bosses.

The route finishes in Whitlingham Country Park, near Trowse. The Broads are Britain's largest protected wetland and this is the newest one, created in recent years from a disused gravel quarry. It has over 280 acres of beautiful countryside, with nature trail walks and cyclepaths through woods and meadows. It offers something for everyone, from walking, cycling and birdwatching to watersports and dry-slope skiing.

Bulrushes abound in this area

ROUTE INFORMATION
National Route: 1
Start: Beccles train station.
Finish: Whitlingham Country Park, near Norwich.
Distance: 24 miles (38.5km).
Grade: Moderate.
Surface: Tarmac paths and minor roads, with a rough section near Whitlingham Country Park, which can be avoided by taking a longer route on roads.
Hills: Mostly flat, with gentle climbs and one steep but short hill.

YOUNG & INEXPERIENCED CYCLISTS
The first stretch of road out of Beccles is the busiest and, although there is a narrow path besides the road, it is not dedicated for use by cyclists. Apart from this, the route is mainly novice-friendly. Its length may be off-putting, however, and a small stretch may be preferable.

Sailing is popular on the Broads

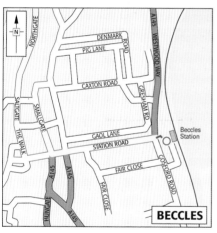

BECCLES

The area is a haven for nature lovers

REFRESHMENTS

- Lots of choice in Beccles.
- The Locks Inn, Geldeston.
- A number of options in Loddon and Chedgrave, including the White Horse pub, Chedgrave.
- Several pubs are passed on the route.
- Cafe in Whitlingham Country Park.
- Lots of choice in Norwich.

THINGS TO SEE & DO

- **Beccles Museum:** magnificent 16th-century building housing a range of exhibits relating to Beccles, surrounding villages and countryside; 01502 715722; www.becclesmuseum.org.uk
- **Loddon and Chedgrave:** ancient market towns worth exploring.
- **Rockland Marshes:** RSPB reserve, with views over Rockland Broad; in spring and summer, kingfishers and great crested grebes can be seen, as well as wetland warblers and barn owls; www.rspb.org.uk
- **Whitlingham Country Park:** cyclepaths, picnic meadow, visitor centre and cafe; 01603 632307; www.broads-authority.gov.uk

TRAIN STATIONS

Beccles.

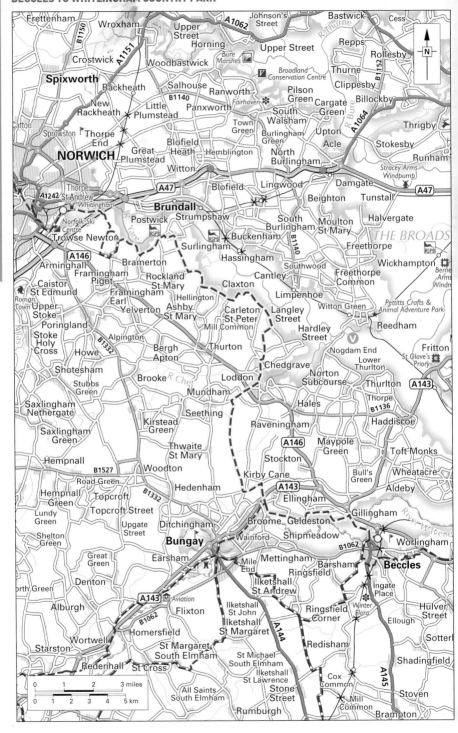

Sailboat on Hickling Broad

BIKE HIRE

- **Martha's Cottage Cycle Hire:** 01502 476789; www.marthascottagecyclehire.co.uk
- **Michael's Cycles, Beccles:** 01502 717413.
- **Outdoor Education Centre, Whitlingham Country Park:** 01603 632307; www.nccoutdooreducation.co.uk

FURTHER INFORMATION

- To view or print National Cycle Network routes, visit www.sustrans.org.uk
- Maps for this area are available to buy from www.sustransshop.co.uk
- **Beccles Tourist Information:** 01502 713196; www.beccles.biz
- **Norfolk Tourist Information:** www.visitnorfolk.co.uk
- **Wherryman's Way:** www.wherrymansway.net

ROUTE DESCRIPTION

From Beccles station, head for the River Waveney, working your way round the one-way system, in the direction of the bus station, where you pick up National Route 1. Continue down Northgate onto Bridge Street and over the river towards Gillingham.

Follow the signposted route until you get to Loddon, where the Wherryman's Way begins. Loddon is an attractive town, with a former

wherry staithe (mooring), a watermill and a 15th-century church. The route takes you neatly into the adjacent village of Chedgrave, where you turn right towards Langley Street.

When you get to Langley, you have the River Yare to your right and the Broads spread out beyond. At Rockland St Mary, you can park your bike and wander past Rockland Broad and out to the River Yare, to sample a wonderful waterside stretch of the Wherryman's Way. Beyond Surlingham, there is a delightful little run-in to the approach to the Country Park.

NEARBY CYCLE ROUTES

National Route 1 continues north on-road to Fakenham, or south from Beccles to Peasenhall and Ipswich. It's part of the Hull to Harwich route and the 3,730-mile (6,000-km) long North Sea Cycle Route, which runs through eight different countries.

The Marriott's Way (see page 114) follows an old railway line from Norwich City to Melton Constable, while the Great Eastern line goes from Wroxham to County School.

Regional Route 31 is signed from Gillingham (near Beccles), where it leaves National Route 1 to Reedham Ferry in Norfolk.

THE MARRIOTT'S WAY

The trail provides an exit from the heart of Norwich into the countryside on one of the longest disused railways in the country. The route is signposted the Wensum Valley Walk from the centre of Norwich and becomes The Marriott's Way near Drayton. William Marriott was the chief engineer and manager of the Midland & Great Northern Joint Railway for an astonishing 41 years. The whole route is studded with a wide variety of broad-leaved trees – oak, ash, hawthorn, silver birch and sycamore. The clear, gently flowing waters of the River Wensum are crossed several times on fine old metal bridges with wooden planking. Between Lenwade and Reepham, you have the option of the full route following the Themelthorpe Loop or taking a shortcut, which saves 4 miles (6.5km) and provides a better surface.

Keep an eye open for the local flora and fauna, as the closure of the railway has been good news for the trackside vegetation and the wildlife that now inhabits it. You may well see jays, magpies, green woodpeckers and wrens. A wide range of plant life, including primroses and wild strawberries, has attracted a rich variety of insects, particularly butterflies and moths. Where the verges are wetter, marsh-marigolds, meadowsweet, Norfolk reeds and horsetail also thrive.

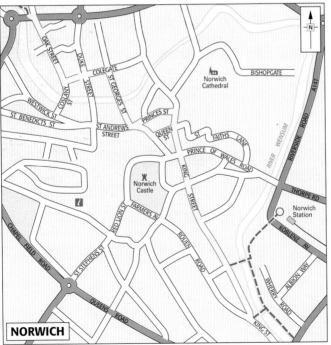

NORWICH

ROUTE INFORMATION

National Route: 1
Start: Norwich train station.
Finish: Reepham market place.
Distance: 15 miles (24km).
Grade: Easy.
Surface: Traffic-free.
Hills: None.

YOUNG & INEXPERIENCED CYCLISTS

Some on-road sections through Norwich where care is required, otherwise traffic-free and flat – great for children just learning to ride!

REFRESHMENTS
- Lots of choice in Norwich.
- A number of options in Drayton and Reepham, including the tearooms at Reepham train station.

THINGS TO SEE & DO
- **Norwich Cathedral:** a Norman cathedral with the second tallest spire in the country; 01603 218300; www.cathedral.org.uk
- **Norwich Castle:** built in the 12th century and now Norfolk's principal museum; 01603 493625; www.museums.norfolk.gov.uk
- **The Lanes:** a network of medieval streets, lanes and alleys with half-timbered houses.
- **Cow Tower, Norwich:** purpose-built artillery blockhouse dating back to 1398; www.english-heritage.org.uk
- **Dinosaur Natural History Park:** Weston Park, Lenwade; 01603 870245; www.dinosauradventure.co.uk
- **Reepham:** a historic town dating back to the 13th century, although the current market dates from the 18th century, with many traditional shops.

TRAIN STATIONS
Norwich.

BIKE HIRE
Enquire locally.

FURTHER INFORMATION
- To view or print National Cycle Network routes, visit www.sustrans.org.uk
- Maps for this area are available to buy from www.sustransshop.co.uk
- **Norwich Tourist Information:** www.visitnorwich.co.uk

ROUTE DESCRIPTION
From Norwich train station, turn left and cross the main road into the Riverside area, with bars, nightclubs and new housing, before crossing the river on a foot/cycle bridge. This

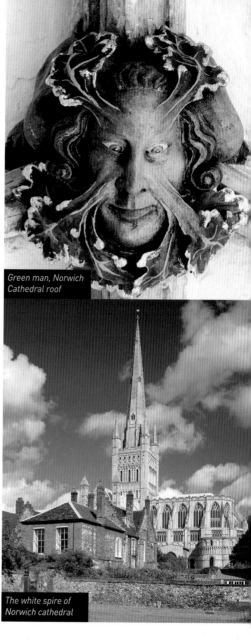

Green man, Norwich Cathedral roof

The white spire of Norwich cathedral

takes you into King Street and the older part of the city. Follow this attractive street to Tombland before following a one-way system to St George Street, Colegate and Oak Street. In Tombland, a short detour will take you to the cathedral, which is well worth a visit. From the centre of Norwich, follow signs for Wensum

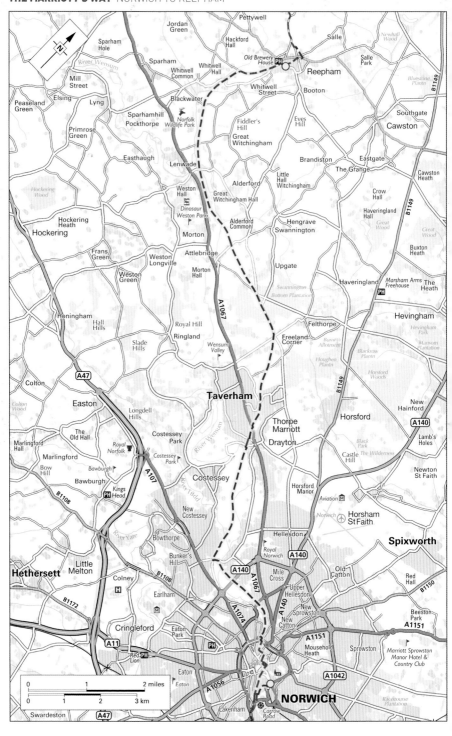

The former Whitwell station, Marriott's Way

Valley Walk, to join the traffic-free path by the River Wensum, which is built on the line of the disused Midland & Great Northern Joint Railway. The path takes you through the woodlands of Mileplain Plantation, which is full of sweet chestnut trees, making the route a special treat in the autumn.

It's not all fields and woods, though, since the path also follows the River Wensum; old metal bridges carry you back and forth across it several times. On the edge of Reepham, Route 1 leaves the disused railway to follow minor roads into the centre of Reepham, where the small market square is well worth a stop. There are several pubs in the village to take a welcome break before the return journey to Norwich.

NEARBY CYCLE ROUTES

National Route 1 continues north on-road to Fakenham, or south from Norwich on-road to Beccles (see page 110). It is part of the Hull to Harwich route and the 3,730-mile (6,000-km) long North Sea Cycle Route, which runs through eight different countries.

The Marriott's Way carries on for another 6 miles (9.5km) east from Reepham to Aylsham, although the surface is not as good as that between Norwich and Reepham. At Aylsham, you can join the Bure Valley Route (unsurfaced) to Wroxham.

CYCLE TO THE WASH – KING'S LYNN TO SNETTISHAM

This route explores the traditional cycling country of west Norfolk. It begins in the bustling town of King's Lynn, an historic medieval port dating back to the 12th century. There is a fascinating old quarter by the river, with handsome Jacobean and Georgian merchants' houses and secretive little yards, evoking the days when it was a busy port. In the hub of it stands the 15th-century Holy Trinity Guildhall, checked with black flint and pale stone, and the former Custom House, which is now home to the Tourist Information Centre. Close by is the Green Quay, an environmental discovery centre, where you can eat in a converted warehouse. The route takes you via the attractive village of Castle Rising, with its impressive 12th-century castle and 17th-century almshouses. Next, you will come to Sandringham Country Park, an area of 620 acres of carefully managed woodland and heath. It has two nature trails and camping and caravan club sites.

If you visit the RSPB's Snettisham reserve, try to do so as a big tide covers the mudflats. Then you will see tens of thousands of wading birds leaving their feeding grounds and moving onto the islands in front of the hides.

For a shorter there-and-back ride, turn around at Castle Rising. This will make the total distance 12 miles (19.5km). Turning back at Sandringham Country Park will give you a 19-mile (30.5-km) round trip.

ROUTE INFORMATION
National Route: 1
Start: King's Lynn train station.
Finish: Shepherd's Port.
Distance: 16 miles (25.5km). Shorter options, from King's Lynn to Castle Rising 6 miles (9.5km); from King's Lynn to Sandringham Country Park 9.5m (15km).
Grade: Easy.

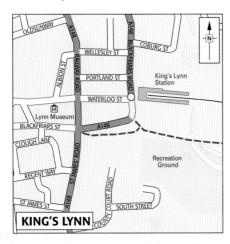

KING'S LYNN

Surface: Tarmac.
Hills: Gentle gradients.

YOUNG & INEXPERIENCED CYCLISTS
The first section is traffic-free, followed by quiet lanes and major roads crossed via central islands, though take particular care crossing the A149.

REFRESHMENTS
- Lots of choice in King's Lynn.
- House on the Green pub, North Wootton.
- Black Horse Inn, Castle Rising.
- Royal Estate visitor centre at Sandringham.
- A number of good pubs in Snettisham, plus the Old Bank Coffee Shop.

THINGS TO SEE & DO
King's Lynn:
- **Custom House:** elegant 17th-century building, with fascinating displays on the merchants, customs men and smugglers; 01553 763044; www.museums.norfolk.gov.uk
- **Town House Museum:** displays the social history and domestic life of Lynn's

King's Lynn's
Custom House

Sandringham House

merchants, traders and families from medieval times to the 1950s; 01553 773450; www.museums.norfolk.gov.uk
- **Lynn Museum:** tells the history of west Norfolk; home to Seahenge, Norfolk's astonishing Bronze Age timber circle; 01553 775001; www.museums.norfolk.gov.uk
- **The Green Quay:** environmental discovery centre, housed in an old Tudor barn; saltwater aquaria with a host of creatures from the Wash; cafe and shop; 01553 818500; www.thegreenquay.co.uk
- **True's Yard Fishing Heritage Museum:** last remaining fishermen's yard in King's Lynn's fishing quarter; fully restored, with a museum, gift shop and tearoom; 01553 770479; www.truesyard.co.uk

Sandringham:
- **Royal Estate at Sandringham:** country retreat of HM the Queen, also includes the country park, museum, visitor centre and 60 acres of stunning gardens; 01553 612908; www.sandringhamestate.co.uk
- **Dersingham Bog National Nature Reserve:** part of the Royal Estate at Sandringham; comprises three distinct habitats: mire, heath and woodland; also home to a rare cuckoo bumblebee; www.naturalengland.org.uk

- **Snettisham Nature Reserve, Shepherd's Port:** the place to witness two of the UK's great wildlife spectacles: tens of thousands of wading birds wheeling over the mudflats, or packed onto roostbanks and islands in front of hides at high tide, plus the skies full of pink-footed geese at dawn and dusk; 01767 680551; www.rspb.org.uk

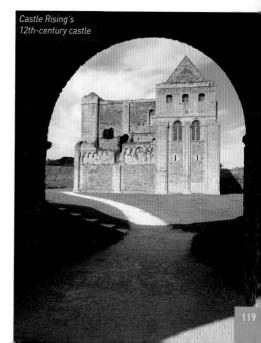

Castle Rising's
12th-century castle

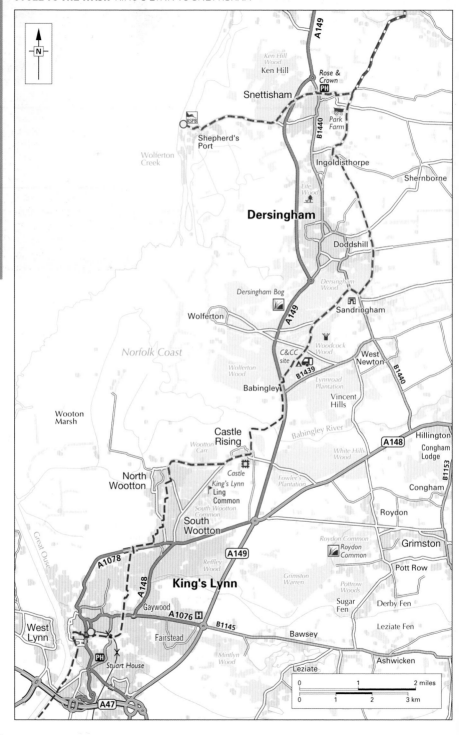

Flock of Red Knot, Snettisham

TRAIN STATIONS

King's Lynn.

BIKE HIRE

- A.E. Wallis, Heacham: 01485 570303; www.aewallis.co.uk

FURTHER INFORMATION

- To view or print National Cycle Network routes, visit www.sustrans.org.uk
- Maps for this area are available to buy from www.sustransshop.co.uk
- King's Lynn Tourist Information: 01553 763044; www.west-norfolk.gov.uk

ROUTE DESCRIPTION

From King's Lynn station forecourt, turn left, following the cycle path besides the main road for a short distance until you arrive at The Walks, a large attractive park. Here, you turn left to join the cyclepath north. After crossing the railway, the route follows a disused railway path, cyclepaths and quiet roads to the edge of North Wootton. Continue on-road through the woodlands of Ling Common, until you come to the attractive village of Castle Rising.You then join a closed road, which takes you onto the cycle track alongside the A149. Ignore the first turn-off for the B1439 and follow the signs for

National Route 1 towards the Royal Estate at Sandringham, crossing the A149 using a central island. The route continues on the road to Snettisham, where this ride leaves the waymarked route and heads westwards for the coast at Shepherd's Port. Take care crossing the A149 again. Be warned that it can be very muddy when the tide is out.

NEARBY CYCLE ROUTES

This route is part of National Route 1 from Hull to Harwich. East from Hunstanton, Route 1 turns inland through Ringstead and Burnham Market to Fakenham, and then on to Harwich via Norwich, Ipswich, Colchester and Felixstowe. West from King's Lynn, it crosses the Fens to Wisbech and Boston. Route 1 continues north from Snettisham to Burnham Market, Wells-next-the-Sea and Fakenham, but doesn't intersect with the rail network again until it reaches Norwich.

The main traffic-free section of Route 1 in this part of the country is The Marriott's Way (see page 114), northwest out of Norwich, one of the flattest National Cycle Network routes.

Regional Route 30, the Norfolk Coast Cycleway, runs from Great Yarmouth through Cromer to King's Lynn. From there it becomes the Two Rivers Route to Lowestoft via Diss.

WELLS & HOLKHAM CIRCUIT

Despite its name, Wells-next-the-Sea is, due to silting, over a mile (1.6km) away from open water. However, it is a delightful fishing port and the perfect base to explore the many delights of the area. Attractions include the Holkham Estate and the Holkham National Nature reserve. Holkham Hall, one of Britain's most majestic stately homes, is a 10-minute ride away along the coast road. The estate welcomes visitors by bicycle, and secure bicycle racks can be found in the Pottery Yard next to the Stables restaurant and the Pottery shop.

You could take a boat trip to Blakeney Point, famous for the colony of common and grey seals you can see basking on the sandbanks. Cley Marshes Nature Reserve, one of the finest bird-watching sites in Britain, is just 10 miles (16km) away. Little Walsingham has been a place of pilgrimage since medieval times and is only 5 miles (8km) away, linked to Wells by a miniature railway similar to that travelling between the town and beach.

Low tide at Wells-Next-the-Sea

ROUTE INFORMATION

National Route: 1
Start and Finish: Harbour at Wells-next-the-Sea.
Distance: 10 miles (16km).
Grade: Medium.
Surface: Mix of private and public roads and paths.
Hills: A couple of testing hills.

YOUNG & INEXPERIENCED CYCLISTS

The route to and from Wells-next-the-Sea uses byways, and some of the surfaces are rough.

REFRESHMENTS

- Lots of choice in Wells-next-the-Sea.
- The Victoria pub, Holkham.

THINGS TO SEE & DO

- **Wells & Walsingham Light Railway:** charming steam railway running throughout the year from Wells to the picturesque town of Walsingham; 4-mile (6.5-km) trip with a journey time of 30 minutes each way; 01328 711630; www.wellswalsinghamrailway.co.uk
- **Holkham Estate:** includes Holkham Hall, a superb Palladian building c.1750; art galleries, museums, food hall, crafts, walking trails and more; 01328 710227; www.holkham.co.uk
- **Holkham National Nature Reserve and Holkham Park:** 9,880 acres of diverse and dramatic nature reserve; maze of creeks and saltings, miles of dunes, shady pinewoods, green pastures and marshes; many rare species of wildlife to be found; 01328 711183; www.holkham.co.uk/naturereserve
- **Blakeney National Nature Reserve:** one of the largest expanses of unspoilt coastline in Europe; vast areas of rare habitats and internationally important breeding area for sea-birds and seals; 01263 740241; www.nationaltrust.org

WELLS-NEXT-THE-SEA

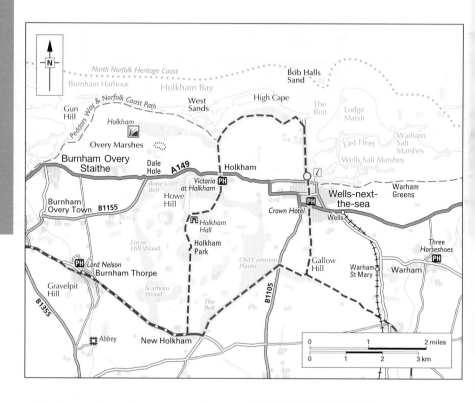

- **Cley Marshes Nature Reserve:** more than 430 acres of varied habitats, from large reedbeds and pools to grazing marshes and meadows; international reputation as a premier birdwatching site; www.norfolkwildlifetrust.org.uk

TRAIN STATIONS
None.

BUSES
Buses run from Sheringham to Hunstanton and vice versa, via Wells-next-the-Sea, and take bikes on board (www.bitternline.com/buses).

BIKE HIRE
- **The Uby Store, Wells-next-the-Sea:** 01328 711054; www.uby7.com

FURTHER INFORMATION
- To view or print National Cycle Network routes, visit www.sustrans.org.uk
- Maps for this area are available to buy from www.sustransshop.co.uk
- Wells-next-the-Sea Tourist Information: 0871 200 3071; www.wells-guide.co.uk
- **West Norfolk Tourist Information:** 01553 763044; www.west-norfolk.gov.uk
- **Norfolk Coast Area of Outstanding Natural Beauty:** www.norfolkcoastaonb.org.uk

ROUTE DESCRIPTION
As this is a circular route, you can go either way to start. To head towards the sea, turn right off The Quay at the harbour and go down Beach Road. Near the end, the route veers left and uses the Norfolk Coast Path, which is a public footpath; pass pedestrians with care.

Cley Marshes

Ruined Little Walsingham Abbey

While the Norfolk Coast Path carries on to the Peddars Way, this route turns inland along Lady Anne's Road towards Holkham. Take care across the A149 and proceed through the gates into Holkham Park – it is undeniably beautiful countryside, and you go through the deer park on your way to Holkham Hall.

This section of the route is all part of the Holkham Estate, and the roads used are courtesy of it, so they may be closed at times. Take the Avenue south beyond the hall, passing the Obelisk. The view back across the park is breathtaking. Exit at South Lodge gates and turn left. Turn left again back along a public road. Turn right at Golden Gate, ignoring the B1105 and follow the signposted track, which can be rough in places.

Turn left towards Wells-next-the-Sea, where you hit Market Lane. Go past the Cuckoo Lodge and turn left at the end onto Burnt Street. Turn right into Plummers Hill and left into Clubbs Lane. At the end, turn left and immediately right into Glebe Road. This takes you back to The Quay at Wells-next-the-Sea harbour.

NEARBY CYCLE ROUTES

This route is part of National Route 1, from Hull to Harwich. West to Hunstanton and King's Lynn, Route 1 crosses the Fens to Wisbech and Boston. It continues southwards from Wells-next-the-Sea to Fakenham.

National Route 13 joins Route 1 at Gateley, near Fakenham. The route continues southwards to Gressenhall, and briefly joins the ancient Peddars Way, a National Trail, and then passes through the market towns of Dereham and Watton, through the edge of Thetford Forest to end at Thetford (see page 86).

Regional Route 30 runs from Great Yarmouth along the coast through Cromer to King's Lynn as the Norfolk Coast Cycleway. From King's Lynn, the route takes an inland route to Lowestoft via Diss as the Two Rivers Route.

The Norfolk Coast Cycleway has various circular routes and links, which follow quiet roads and lanes through varied countryside between King's Lynn and Great Yarmouth via Cromer.

NEXT STEPS...

We hope you have enjoyed the cycle rides in this book.

Sustrans developed the National Cycle Network to act as a catalyst for bringing cycling (and walking) back into our everyday lives. Between the 1950s and the mid 1970s cycling in the UK fell by 80%. Cycling now accounts for only about 2% of all journeys made in the UK, a fraction of what we used to achieve.

When you consider that nearly 6 in 10 car journeys are under 5 miles, it makes you wonder what the potential for increasing levels of cycling is? Evidence shows that, for local journeys under 5 miles, the majority of us could make 9 out of 10 journeys on foot, bike or public transport if there was more investment in making it possible to choose to leave the car behind.

And why not? We can all be more savvy when it comes to travel. One small step becomes one giant leap if we all start walking away from less healthy lifestyles and pedalling our way towards happier children and a low carbon world.

And that's where Sustrans comes in. Sustainable travel means carbon-reducing, energy efficient, calorie burning, money-saving travel. Here are a few things that we think make sense. If you agree, join us.

- **Snail's pace** – 20 mph or less on our streets where we live, go to school, shop and work – make it the norm, not just the four times a century when we get snow.

- **Closer encounters** – planning that focuses on good non-motorised access, so that we can reach more post offices, schools, shops, doctors and dentists without the car.

- **People spaces** – streets where kids can play hopscotch or football and be free-range, and where neighbours can meet and chat.

- **Road revolution** – build miles and miles of bike paths that don't evaporate when they meet a road.

- **Find our feet** – campaign for pedestrian-friendly city centres, or wide boulevards with regular pedestrian crossings and slow-moving traffic.

- **Better buses** – used by millions, under-invested by billions and, if affordable, reliable and pleasant to use, could make local car journeys redundant.

- **More car clubs** – a car club on every street corner and several for every new-build estate.

- **Rewards for car-sharing** – get four in a car and take more than half the cars off the road.

- **Trains** – more of them, more cheaply.

- **Become a staycationer** – and holiday at home. Mountains, beaches, culture, great beer, good food and a National Cycle Network that connects them all.

If we work towards these goals we have a chance of delivering our fair share of the 80% reduction in CO_2 by mid-century that we're now committed to by law, and some of the 100% reduction that many climate experts now consider essential.

Help Sustrans to change our world

Join the charity that is making a difference today so we can all live a better tomorrow.

Sustrans is the UK's leading sustainable transport charity. Our vision is a world in which people choose to travel in ways that benefit their health and the environment. We are the charity working with children in schools, with families at home, with employers and with whole communities to enable people to travel much more by foot, bike and public transport. Sustrans is a 'doing' charity; working with many partners to bring about real change. Our thousands of supporters are enabling and helping us to change our world one mile at a time. You can too.

Join the movement today at www.sustrans.org.uk/support

Or call 0845 838 0651

sus**trans**
JOIN THE MOVEMENT

ACKNOWLEDGEMENTS

Vincent Cassar would like to thank Sustrans Rangers in the East of England, including Richard Arthurs, Andrew Bowen, Chris Chorley, Terry Colver, David Johnson, Sue Flower, Pam Nelson, John Pitts, Stephen Read, Peter Robertson, Keith Scott, Richard Simpson, Frank Turner and Jonathan Webster.

The Automobile Association wishes to thank the following photographers and organisations for their assistance in the preparation of this book.

Abbreviations for the picture credits are as follows – (t) top; (b) bottom; (l) left; (r) right; (c) centre; (dps) double page spread; (AA) AA World Travel Library

Trade Cover: t Stranded boats at Wells-next-the-Sea, Norfolk, AA/T Mackie; b Smiling girl, Jon Bewley/ Sustrans

Special Sales Cover: t Boats along the River Stour in Dedham, Suffolk, AA/T Mackie; b Young couple cycling through a meadow, Digital Vision/Getty

3l Jon Bewley; 3r AA/C Coe; 4 Wellcome Trust; 5 Katy Hallett/Sustrans; 6/7 AA/T Mackie; 7t AA/T Mackie; 7c AA/T Mackie; 7b AA/J Miller; 11tl Jon Bewley/ Sustrans; 11tr Jon Bewley/Sustrans; 11c Jon Bewley/ Sustrans; 11bc Andy Huntley/Sustrans; 11br Pru Comben/Sustrans; 13t Jon Bewley/Sustrans; 13c Nicola Jones/Sustrans; 13b Jon Bewley/Sustrans; 14 Sustrans; 15 Sustrans; 17t Sustrans; 17b Sustrans; 19 AA/C Jones; 21t AA/W Voysey; 21c Sustrans; 23 © Tony Eveling/Alamy; 24 AA/M Birkitt; 25t AA/M Birkitt; 25c © Travelpix/Alamy; 27t © G Owston (Hertfordshire)/Alamy; 27c AA/N Setchfield; 28t AA/N Setchfield; 28c AA/N Setchfield; 31l © Joe Wardman/ Alamy; 31r Owned by the Harlow Art Trust, image copyright: Graham Portlock; 31c © Tony Eveling/ Alamy; 32 Owned by the Harlow Art Trust, image copyright: Graham Portlock; 33t Sustrans; 33c Sustrans; 34 © Seren Digital:Essex Life/Alamy;

35 AA/W Voysey; 37 © Seren Digital:Essex Life/Alamy; 38/39 Photolibrary Group; 39t Sustrans; 41 AA/N Hicks; 43 AA/M Birkitt; 45t AA/M Moody; 45c AA/C Jones; 47 © Martin Bond/Alamy; 48 © Colin Palmer Photography/Alamy; 49t AA/C Jones; 49c Colin Palmer Photography/Alamy; 50 © CountrySideCollection - Homer Sykes/Alamy; 51t AA/ J Miller; 51c © Greg Balfour Evans/Alamy; 53 AA/J Miller; 55 AA/R Surnam; 56 AA/T Mackie; 59 © John Woodworth/Alamy; 61 AA/J Miller; 62/63 © Michael Jones/Alamy; 63 AA/T Mackie; 65 © Jon Crwys- Williams/Alamy; 66 AA/R Surnam; 67 © geogphotos/ Alamy; 69 AA/T Mackie; 70 © www.janelewis.co.uk/ Alamy; 71t John Grimshaw; 71b © Mark Pink/Alamy; 73 © Adams Picture Library t/a apl/Alamy; 74 AA/T Woodcock; 74/75 AA/M Moody; 77t AA/M Birkitt; 77b © Tom Mackie/Alamy; 78 AA/C Coe; 79tl Katy Hallett/ Sustrans; 79tr AA/C Coe; 81t AA/M Birkitt; 81b Katy Hallett/Sustrans; 83t © Alistair Laming/Alamy; 83c AA/R Surman; 85l © Robert Estall photo agency/ Alamy; 85r © David J. Green - Bury St Edmunds/ Alamy; 86/87 AA/S & O Mathews; 89 AA/M Moody; 90/91 AA/T Mackie; 91 AA/M Birkitt; 93 AA/T Mackie; 94 Sustrans; 95 © Mark Pink/Alamy; 97 AA/J Tims; 99t © Bildarchiv Monheim GmbH/Alamy; 99b © Darrin Jenkins/Alamy; 101 AA/S & O Mathews; 102/103 AA/M Birkitt; 103 AA/D Hall; 105 © Rod Edwards/Alamy; 106/107 © T.M.O.Landscapes/Alamy; 109 © geogphotos/Alamy; 110 AA/T Mackie; 111t AA/T Mackie; 111c AA/T Mackie; 113 AA/T Mackie; 115t © Holmes Garden Photos/Alamy; 115b AA/T Mackie; 117 © Clive Tully/Alamy; 119tl © Angelo Hornak/Alamy; 119tr AA/T Mackie; 119b AA/R J Edwards; 121 © Andrew Darrington/Alamy; 122/123 AA/T Mackie; 125l AA/A J Hopkins; 125r AA/M Birkitt

Every effort has been made to trace the copyright holders, and we apologise in advance for any unintentional omissions or errors. We would be pleased to apply any corrections in the following edition of this publication.